The Underground Railroad in Bedford County Pennsylvania

Kevin Mearkle

Cover: Photograph of the Imes Cemetery near Chaneysville, Pennsylvania - October 2023

Authors previous books: Civil War Soldiers of Bedford County Pennsylvania (2021)
Battlefield Tour Guide of Bedford County Soldiers at Gettysburg and Antietam (2022)

Harriette Bradley is pictured with her son David Bradley, and husband, Reverend David H. Bradley. The research efforts of Harriette Bradley are often referenced in this book. The photograph is from a Bedford Gazette article on February 7th, 1956. (Bedford County Historical Society)

This book is dedicated to those who first provided the information contained in these pages. Their efforts enabled this story on the Underground Railroad to be told.

*The Underground Railroad
in
Bedford County Pennsylvania*

First Edition
IngramSpark Publishing Company

Copyright © 2023 Kevin Mearkle

All rights reserved. No portion of this book may be reproduced in any form without permission from the author, except as permitted by U.S. copyright law.

For permission requests contact: kevinmearklehistory@gmail.com

Contents

	Dedication	iii
1.	Introduction	1
2.	Overview	3
3.	Origins	5
4.	Fugitive Slave Legislation	9
5.	Early Black History in Bedford County	13
6.	A Divisive Time	19
7.	Geography and Transportation	23
8.	North Star	29
9.	Cumberland Maryland	31
10.	Chaneysville	37
11.	Bloody Run and Rainsburg	45
12.	Cumberland Valley	55
13.	Bedford	63
14.	The Path to Harpers Ferry went through Bedford	73
15.	Snake Spring Valley, Woodbury, and Bloomfield Township	81
16.	Fishertown and Pleasantville	89
17.	Conclusion	101
	Acknowledgements	103
	Notes	105
	Bibliography	119
	Index	121

Maps

Cumberland, Maryland area	28
Bedford County area	35

Sources for photographs or images are in parentheses except those provided by the author.

The Underground Railroad
(Cincinnati Art Museum)

This iconic painting of an Underground Railroad scene by Charles Webber was viewed for the first time at the Columbian World's Fair in Chicago in 1893. The image shows a family of enslaved people arriving at the home of Levi Coffin. Coffin was one of the most well-known Underground Railroad agents of the era. One of the people who viewed this painting in Chicago was Wilbur H. Siebert, who had met Levi Coffin in 1847. Siebert was deeply moved by this image and was inspired to write one of the seminal books on the Underground Railroad published in 1898. Wilbur Siebert reached out to the mayor of Bedford, requesting recollections for the book he was writing. John W. Rouse, son of a famed Underground Railroad agent, responded with two remarkable letters in 1895 detailing efforts in Bedford County. The contents of these letters are reviewed in the Cumberland Valley and Bedford chapters of this book.

Chapter 1
Introduction

Geography and transportation often placed Bedford County Pennsylvania at the crossroads of early American History. Few rural areas have hosted the range of historical figures or witnessed the breadth of significant events. The Pennsylvania Historical Museum Commission sponsored a study of the Underground Railroad. The following excerpts from the study cite the symbolic significance of the movement and note the exodus of runaways that crossed the Bedford County border.

> It is hard to dispute that fugitive slaves were at the center of the national crisis that led to the Civil War. Escaping slaves helped fuel the growing sectionalism, as both sides disagreed, sometimes violently, over how to deal with the problem of recovering human property. Of all the counties in southwestern Pennsylvania, Bedford County probably had the most active free black population and rigorous Underground Railroad traffic. [1]

A convergence of factors influenced the flow of freedom seekers into the county. Two slave states were nearby. Bedford County is on the Maryland state line, and Virginia was less than 10 miles from the county border prior to the Civil War. In 1863, West Virginia split away from Virginia, forming a new state.

Cumberland Maryland was a major transportation hub during the Underground Railroad era. The first federally funded road in America, the National Road (Route 40), ran through Cumberland and connected Baltimore to the Ohio River. One of the first railroad lines in America, the Baltimore & Ohio, maintained a bustling station in Cumberland. The C&O Canal linked Cumberland with Washington, DC. [2] Blacks helped build all three and transported goods along its routes after completion.

Topography factored into the flow of runaways. Many enslaved people could not read or write, and few had access to maps or a compass. Most were aware the Appalachian Mountains pointed in a northern direction. The rugged mountain ridges and wooded rolling hills of the region provided ample cover for freedom seekers wanting to remain unseen.

Bedford County had a thriving black population prior to the Civil War. The 1850 and 1860 census reports listed over 400 free black people in Bedford County. Some were born into slavery, others were the sons and daughters of enslaved people, and limited numbers were born to parents who were born free; many helped enslaved people seeking freedom. [3]

Over time, a loose network of white and black supporters of enslaved people formed to serve as guides and provide refuge in secretive hideouts throughout Bedford County. Primary source documents written by people who took part in or witnessed an Underground Railroad event are limited. Wilbur H. Siebert, a leading historian and author of the seminal book, "The Underground Railroad from Slavery to Freedom," noted the following in 1898.

> It is not surprising, in view of the unlawful nature of Underground Railroad service, that extremely little in the way of contemporaneous documents has descended to us even across the short span of a generation or two, and that there are few written data for the history of a movement that gave liberty to thousands of slaves. [4]

The Fugitive Slave Act of 1850 increased the penalties for aiding or harboring freedom seekers. Those caught were subject to a fine of $1000, six months in jail, and additional civil liabilities. [5] The penalties were harsh. One thousand dollars in 1850 is the equivalent of $38,355 in 2023. [6] Despite the personal risks, Bedford County residents helped substantial numbers of enslaved people. Only two individuals have numbers attributed to their efforts. Reverend John Fidler of Bedford was credited with helping hundreds, possibly more than a thousand, runaways gain freedom. [7] Benjamin H. Walker, a conductor in the Quaker community near Pleasantville, was cited for helping over 500 runaways. [8] Many other supporters of the Underground Railroad in Bedford County aided unknown numbers of freedom seekers.

A cloak of secrecy prevented much of the story from being documented. Supporters were careful not to leave paper trails of activities while the Underground Railroad operated. Few wrote about their efforts after it concluded. Much of what exists is tantalizing bits of information, passed along by word of mouth, and documented decades after the Underground Railroad ended. These stories have been retold in newspapers, local history books, historical papers, and event brochures. This book compiles what has been written and references where it was first documented.

Limited original source documentation creates challenges in researching the subject. The Underground Railroad ended over 150 years ago. Discovery of new original source materials necessary to corroborate some details appears unlikely. There are many known unknowns in the story of the Underground Railroad. The total number of freedom seekers who passed through Bedford County will never be known. The identities of some who helped others gain freedom have been lost to history. Verification of some details is not possible, and some questions will remain unanswered. Few options exist beyond accessing the sources of information and evaluating if a story fits within the context of what is known. This book acknowledges these realities.

The Bedford County story of the Underground Railroad illustrates the best in human nature and the worst in humanity. It is a story of courageous people risking bodily harm, fleeing into an unfamiliar world and uncertain future. It is a story of kind people risking incarceration and financial ruin to help strangers they would never meet again. It is also a story of despicable individuals who pursued freedom seekers for financial gain and those who tipped off the slave catchers for a share of the reward.

This book examines some of the inflection points leading up to the Civil War and the Bedford County connection to these events. Four months before the Harpers Ferry raid, John Brown met with three Bedford abolitionists. What is known about Brown's stay in Bedford County and the ill-fated raid that fanned the flames of succession are detailed in chapter 14 - The Path to Harpers Ferry went through Bedford. Bedford County connections to one of the most consequential Supreme Court cases in American history, the Dred Scott Decision, are covered in chapter 4 - Fugitive Slave Legislation.

Many of the locations cited in the Underground Railroad stories of Bedford County are identified, including an unexpected number of structures still standing today. Verbatim excerpts of original and initial source materials are referenced to allow an unedited evaluation of what has been written. More than a century and a half after it ceased to exist, the Underground Railroad remains an unusually compelling story.

Chapter 2
Overview

The following are some commonly used terms, concepts, and practical workings of the Underground Railroad. Supporters who helped runaways were often referred to as agents, engineers, and conductors. An agent was a broader term for someone who provided aid of any type. Some agents made financial contributions to those who harbored or helped transport runaways. Others passed along useful information, including the whereabouts of people pursuing freedom seekers.

Stations, also referred to as safe houses, were spaced at convenient distances along various routes north. Freedom seekers were provided food, shelter, clothing, directions, and money at stations. Slave catchers watched for enslaved people along known routes and were occasionally hot on the trail of runaways. People running stations made themselves available to receive runaways, anytime day or night. Freedom seekers hid in houses, barns, sheds, churches, business structures, and outside locations near stations. Secrecy was important. Those aiding runaways were concerned about the prying eyes of neighbors. Unfamiliar people seen on properties could raise suspicions. Even neighbors sympathetic to the plight of enslaved people could spread rumors. Freedom seekers remained at a station for varying amounts of time until deemed safe to proceed to the next station.

During the early era of the Underground Railroad, most enslaved runaways were men traveling by themselves. After receiving aid, most were provided detailed directions and proceeded alone to the next station. Guides accompanied enslaved people only during special circumstances. Over time, guides between stations became necessary. More women and children began seeking freedom, families traveling together became common, and pursuing slave catchers more frequent. [1]

The following are excerpts from a story written in 1890 by William Maclay Hall, a retired judge in Bedford. He provides some interesting color on the slave catchers who prowled the hills and mountains in Bedford County.

> The fugitives followed the mountains which run northwardly, and the slave catchers lay in wait, both by day and night, at the crossing places of the roads, and arrests were made without any warrant or process of law. Negroes and mulattoes were captured and bound and conducted back to their owners or to slave catchers in Maryland. The slave-hunters of Bedford County, the men who received and posted the handbills and got the rewards, were looked down upon and despised by their neighbors. The slave catchers were, for the most part, a despicable set: they were men who drank whisky, chewed tobacco, played cards, and loafed around village taverns. Occasionally, however, there was a farmer or mechanic who was sneakingly engaged in the business. Each community in the southern part of the county contained them. The little knot of them in Bedford borough were well known forty years ago. They are all dead now, with a single exception. [2]

Conductor was a term used for a person who provided transportation or served as a guide. Circumstances dictated how and when conductors helped enslaved people reach the next station. Travel was sometimes judged less risky under the cover of darkness. Other times, freedom seekers were transported in broad daylight. Many were concealed in wagons and closed carriages. Wagons often transported crops, produce, and store goods to avoid suspicion. Conductors often had a choice of proceeding to various stations. Underground Railroad routing resembled more of a zigzag than a straight line. The flexibility helped to throw slave catchers off the trails of enslaved runaways. A myriad of deceptions were often employed during travel to thwart pursuers. [3]

Freedom seekers often traveled with forged, borrowed, or stolen documents. Enslaved people in the south were required to carry travel documents or passes. Free blacks in southern states had papers with clear descriptions stating they were not enslaved. Disguises were often used to avoid suspicion or recognition from a description on a fugitive handbill or newspaper advertisement. [4]

Steam railroads became a more common mode of transportation in the 1850s. No documentation has been found of a runaway boarding a train in Bedford County. Stories exist of freedom seekers boarding trains in Blair and Cambria counties. The newspaper article on the right "A Slave Stampede" describes one daring steam railroad escape. Four females and one male seized two horses and a buggy and fled across the Pennsylvania border. They boarded a train in Chambersburg bound for Harrisburg and freedom. [5]

Agents developed various figurative phrases, codes, and signals. Examples include a distinctive number of knocks on the door or a conductor's reply of being, "a friend with friends." When freedom seekers traveled alone, a specific password or code phrase was often used. A church bell in Cumberland, MD, served as a signal. When an agent rang the bell in a coded way, runaways knew it was safe to proceed. [6]

Some exceedingly rare records on freedom seekers were kept by one organization. The Vigilance Committee of Philadelphia was formed in the 1830s to help enslaved people. The committee raised funds to provide boarding, clothing, medical attention, legal counsel, and guidance north. Records kept by this organization provide interesting insights on the enslaved runaways who streamed into southeastern Pennsylvania. These findings apply to other areas in the state, including Bedford County. An overwhelming majority of enslaved people came from Virginia, Maryland, Washington D.C., and Delaware. Few came from large plantations. Most were involved in a trade. Occasionally, enslaved people traveled together, sometimes in groups as large as a couple dozen men, women, and children. A fair number of freedom seekers carried arms or knives. Almost all had to purchase transportation or food during their journey. A significant majority involved elaborate deceptions, including false identities or forged travel documents. [7]

Agents needed courage, fortitude, and guile to conduct operations on the Underground Railroad. A strong moral compass and a firm sense of purpose were common virtues. The runaways risked considerable physical harm if caught. No small amount of courage, determination, and spirit was necessary to persevere during a journey to freedom. [8]

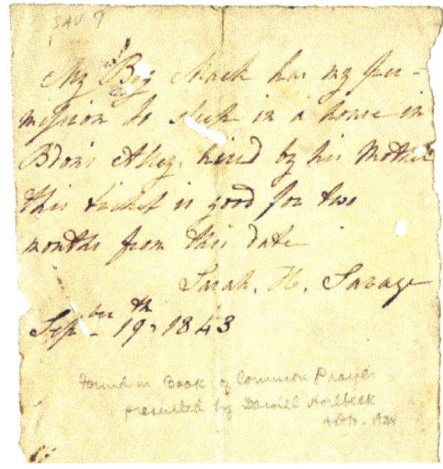

1843 slave pass.
(College of Charleston Libraries)

Herald of Freedom & Torch Light, Hagerstown, MD - 27 May 1857.
(Western MD. Historical Library)

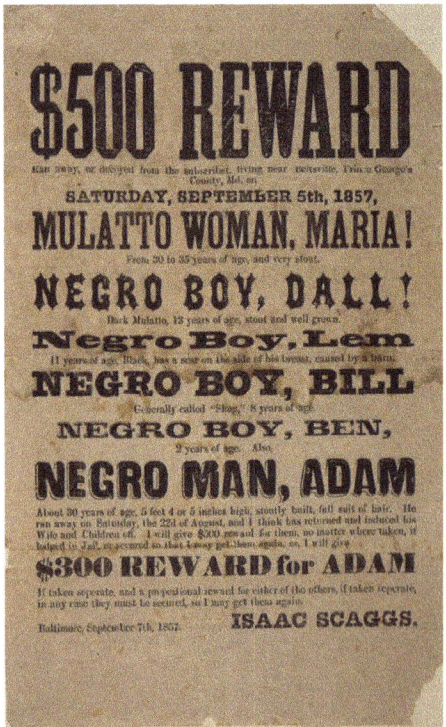

1857 handbill in Prince George's County, MD. (for sale on the internet)

Chapter 3

Origins

The origins of the Underground Railroad movement are unclear. People fleeing slavery predated the founding of the United States of America. In the 1650s, Maryland negotiated regulations on the return of enslaved people from New Netherland. New Netherland was a Dutch province that included parts of Delaware, Pennsylvania, New Jersey, New York, and Connecticut. [1]

The origins of the term - Underground Railroad are uncertain. Different folklore narratives emerged over time. One often recited story occurred in 1831. A runaway, Tice Davids swam across the Ohio River with an enslaver in close pursuit. When the enslaver reached the other side of the river, Tice Davids was nowhere to be found. The frustrated enslaver muttered the runaway must have "gone off on an underground road." The story was retold with much amusement. [2] The wording may have changed from "underground road" to "underground railroad" as railroads became a transformational innovation of the era. The term Underground Railroad began appearing in Abolitionist journals and newspapers in the 1840s. [3]

George Washington cited enslaved people being aided by organized groups in two letters written in 1786. In a May 12th letter, Washington wrote an enslaved person of another man in Alexandria had escaped to Philadelphia. He noted, "a society of Quakers in the city, formed for such purposes, attempted to liberate" the enslaved runaway. A second letter written on November 20th stated: "there are numbers (of people) who would rather facilitate the escape of slaves than apprehend them when runaways." Washington appears to believe Philadelphia in general, and the Quakers in particular, were supportive of efforts to free enslaved people. [4]

In 1775, a group of Philadelphia Quakers led by Anthony Benezet founded the "Society for the Relief of Free Negroes Unlawfully Held in Bondage." The organization was the first anti-slavery society in America. [5] Benjamin Rush, a signer of the Declaration of Independence, helped to raise money for black churches in Philadelphia. Both the Mother Bethel African Methodist Episcopal (AME) Church and The African Episcopal Church of St. Thomas were founded in 1794. [6]

A reference to an enslaved runaway near the Bedford County border took place in 1803. An enslaver in Oldtown Maryland, south of Flintstone, offered a reward in the Frederick Town Herald. A man named Anthony reportedly fled with a considerable quantity of clothing. The advertisement ran for three months. [7]

By 1804, clandestine efforts to help enslaved people were taking place in Lancaster County, Pennsylvania. Townspeople in Columbia began intervening on behalf of runaways after cases of kidnapping became known. Soon after, efforts to aid enslaved people spread to Quaker communities in York, Chester, Montgomery, Berks, and Bucks Counties. [8]

Canada became known as a refuge for freedom seekers during the War of 1812. Returning soldiers told stories of the Canadian government defending the rights of self-emancipated black people. [9] By

Frederick Town Herald - September 17th, 1803. (MD State Archives)

1815, stories emerged of runaways reaching Canada, aided by sympathetic people in Ohio. Abolitionists began venturing south, under the guise of business dealings, to circulate information on routes to Canada. Some courageous freedom seekers returned from Canada to rescue family and friends. These heroic actions substantiated the rumors of Canada being a sanctuary and sowed the seeds of hope for enslaved people longing for freedom. [10]

The Frederick Town Herald newspaper ran an advertisement in 1819 offering a $100 reward for the return of an Allegany County, Maryland runaway. The advertisement stated a Patrick Smith, about 18 or 19 years of age, may have gone to Bedford, where he has an acquaintance. It is unknown if the runaway was ever captured. [11]

The Kernel of Greatness bicentennial book noted a story of enslaved runaways being apprehended in Bedford County in 1825. Two freedom seekers named George and Harry were seized by slave catchers and returned to Fauquier County, Virginia. [12]

In 1828, an enslaver in Loudon County, Virginia, placed an advertisement in the Bedford Democratic Enquirer, shown on the next page. George and Mary Love offered a $100 reward for a runaway named Richard Gant. The advertisement detailed a physical description, clothing last worn, and noted the runaway chews tobacco, smokes, and is fond of ardent spirits (presumably whiskey). The enslavers suspected Richard Gant may have assumed a new identity on counterfeit travel pass papers. [13]

1819 Frederick Town Herald ad mentions Bedford as possible destination. (Maryland State Archives)

Abolitionists in border states reported the number of runaways fleeing slavery accelerated in the 1830s.[14] These observations coincided with an increase in newspaper advertisements offering rewards for runaways in Cumberland, Maryland, newspapers. Bedford is mentioned in an advertisement titled "Fifty Dollars Reward" published in the Maryland Advocate is shown on the next page. This advertisement ran on the front page of the Maryland Advocate on June 4th, 1833. [15]

. The Underground Railroad had grown into a widespread movement in northern states by the 1840s. In February 1846, a newspaper in Hagerstown, Maryland stated, "it is very evident to our minds, that the abolitionists of the North have some sort of secret influences at work amongst the slaves in Maryland and Virginia." [16]

The 1850s were the most active period in the north, according to consensus opinions of those involved in the Underground Railroad. [17] The passage of the Fugitive Slave Act of 1850 preceded this increase in activity. A series of fugitive slave laws likely contributed to the expansion of the Underground Railroad north of the Mason-Dixon line. William P. Shell also noted Fugitive Slave laws increased the number of people pursuing freedom seekers. The following are some of his recollections published in a 1906 Bedford Gazette article.

> The effect of these laws was to create a class of slave catchers who, for the sake of the reward generally offered for the apprehension of the fugitives, pursued the poor, unfortunate slaves with the ferocity of hounds and with the ardor and zest of the catchers of horse thieves. All this was cruel and shameful enough, but there was no compulsion on any citizen to aid in the capture. But the friends of the poor fugitives also increased, and they were equal to the emergency. For their kind and humane treatment of the slaves, they deserve the praise of men and the blessing of God. [18]

Enslaved people crossing the Bedford County border did not end with the outbreak of the Civil War. The following is a verbatim transcription of an Altoona Tribune article published in April 1862. No additional information was found on Spriggs, the slave catcher referenced in the story.

Considerable excitement has been created in this place and Hollidaysburg, arising out of an

Chapter 3 - Origins 7

This highly descriptive reward advertisement ran in the Democratic Enquirer, a Bedford newspaper on May 14th, 1828. It details the physical attributes and habits of Richard Gant. The enslaver mentioned the possibility of Gant changing his identity and traveling with a counterfeit travel pass or papers stating he was a free black. (Bible, Ax, and Plow)

Maryland Advocate in Cumberland, Maryland, ran this ad on June 4th, 1833. Sam, the enslaved man, was married to a free black who had gone to visit her mother in Bedford two weeks earlier. The 1836 post stamped date on the bottom left of the ad is believed to be incorrect. (Western Maryland's Historical Library)

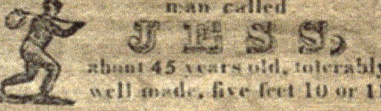

(above) Reward advertisement ran in the Maryland Advocate on March 12th, 1833. The date - Feb 5, 1833, at the bottom, may have been when the ad was first placed. (Western Maryland's Historical Library)

(left) Maryland Advocate in Cumberland, Maryland, ran this reward advertisement on November 20th, 1832. (Western Maryland's Historical Library)

attempt to arrest some three or four fugitive slaves and an alleged horse thief, from the vicinity of Cumberland, Maryland, The truth of the matter is hard to get at, owing to the different stories, in circulation. As far as we can learn, it stands about thus: On Monday morning last, a man named Spriggs came to this place and requested Constable Ely to assist him in arresting some horse-thieves. He stated that a party of colored men had stolen a horse near Cumberland, came to Bedford and sold him, and hired a conveyance to bring them from Bedford to Hollidaysburg. While the Constable and Spriggs were talking, the party came suddenly around a corner, whereupon Ely proceeded to arrest them. He succeeded in securing one of them, and a woman who was with the party, but three of them made their escape. They were pursued out of town by a party of some ten or twelve men, but were not overtaken. It turned out afterwards that the man arrested was a freeman, and that the three that escaped were slaves. The man and woman arrested were taken to Hollidaysburg and placed in jail. The excitement created by the arrest ran pretty high in this place for some time - a number alleging that Spriggs did not have warrant, and had no authority to arrest any of the party, while others contended that he had a right to his slaves, and applied the term "Abolitionist" pretty freely to those who argued against the proceedings. At the instance of some of the colored men of this place, the man and woman were brought before Judge Moses, on Tuesday last, on a writ of *habeas corpus* - E. Hammond, appearing for Spriggs, and Messrs. Calvin and Dean for the defendants. In the opinion of the Judge, the evidence was not sufficient to hold them, and they were accordingly dismissed. We have been informed that there was a large crowd of white and colored people around the jail when the prisoners were liberated, and that for a time there were strong symptoms of a riot - pistols and knives being freely shown, and a demand made for clubs and stones. The prisoners finally got out of the crowd and left for other parts.

Not knowing all the circumstances connected with the case, we shall venture no opinion in reference to the proceedings of the officers of the law, or the crowds, either here or at Hollidaysburg, but will simply give the different versions as they have been given us. Those who wished to have the men arrested allege that Spriggs is the owner of the slaves and a loyal Union man, and that the horse left at Bedford was stolen and sold, thus making them horse-thieves as well as slaves. The opposite party allege that Spriggs is only a "nigger-catcher" from Bedford; that he had no authority to arrest the party either as slaves or horse-thieves; that they did not sell the horse at Bedford, but paid for his keeping and ordered him sent back to Cumberland at the first opportunity. Here the matter rests for the present, but it has, doubtless, broken friendships which it will require many years to renew and done injuries to men that will require time to overcome.[19]

After the Civil War ended, the Underground Railroad movement faded into history. Bedford County supporters quietly moved on with their lives. Many mourned loved ones lost during the war. Few would ever write about efforts to help enslaved people gain freedom. Some stories, initially passed along by word of mouth, have survived.

Chapter 4
Fugitive Slave Legislation

The Commonwealth of Pennsylvania first passed abolition legislation in 1780, while the American colonies were fighting for their own freedom in the Revolutionary War. The Gradual Abolition Act of 1780 contained wording condemning the tyranny of Great Britain and equating British oppression to slavery. [1]

As the name suggests, the Gradual Abolition legislation did not immediately end slavery in Pennsylvania. To gain support for passage, opponents in Lancaster and Chester counties insisted on ending slavery gradually. The law required enslaved people to be registered; non-compliance resulted in the person being set free. Further importation of slavery was illegal. Enslaved people brought to Pennsylvania by a non-resident could stay no longer than 6 months. Previously enacted legislation discriminating against free blacks was voided. One clause perpetuated slavery longer than envisioned by legislators. The children of enslaved people could be registered as servants until age 28. [2] The vague wording of this clause led to interpretations that children born to women who were registered as servants could also be registered as servants until age 28. [3]

In the colonial era, many Europeans agreed to become indentured servants for a set time in exchange for transportation costs to America or an apprenticeship. [4] Generally, indentured servitude was a voluntary agreement. A key difference exists between indentured servitude and the registration of children as servants until age 28. The term registration of children was not voluntary.

The 1793 Fugitive Slave Act sought to address festering controversies with southern slave states. This federal law established the right of enslavers to arrest alleged runaways and present evidence in court. A warrant was issued for the return of an escaped freedom seeker if the court ruled in favor of the enslaver. After a warrant was issued, those hindering, rescuing, or harboring an enslaved person were subject to a fine of $500 and imprisonment for up to a year. [5]

The 1826 Pennsylvania Personal Liberty Law criminalized the act of free blacks being taken or lured out of PA to be enslaved. Other provisions in the legislation sought to ensure fair treatment of freedom seekers in the court system, including a requirement of testimony from a neutral person.[6]

In 1842, the U.S. Supreme Court ruled the 1826 Pennsylvania Personal Liberty Law was unconstitutional. The Prigg v. Pennsylvania decision reversed the conviction of slave catcher Edward Prigg, establishing the primacy of federal fugitive slave legislation over state personal liberty laws. Details of the Prigg v. Pennsylvania case centered on the wife and children of a free black man in Pennsylvania being kidnapped. Margaret Morgan claimed her freedom had been granted by a deceased enslaver in Maryland, unfortunately no documentation existed. The estate of the enslaver hired Edward Prigg to abduct Margaret and her children in Pennsylvania. The Prigg decision affirmed the right of enslavers to arrest escaped runaways and delegated authority to the U.S. Congress to enforce the law. [7] Northern states reacted by passing new personal liberty laws to weaken the Prigg decision, further infuriating southern slave states.

The Pennsylvania Personal Liberty law enacted in early 1847 prohibited state and local law enforcement from pursuing freedom seekers. Slave catchers were also denied the use of jails to hold enslaved people. In March 1847, a Hagerstown, Maryland newspaper accused Pennsylvania of "agitating" over the right of enslavers to reclaim escaped runaways. In June 1847, a prominent enslaver in Hagerstown, James H. Kennedy, went to Carlisle with several others to reclaim 10 to 12 enslaved people. A mob of free black people fatally wounded Kennedy, while white residents stood by. This incident touched off a bitter controversy between the two states. Maryland legislators passed a resolution demanding Pennsylvania repeal the recently enacted Personal Liberty Law. The Pennsylvania legislature ignored the request. [8]

Fugitive Slave Act of 1850 became known as the "Great Compromise." Free and slave states had maintained a delicate balance of power arrangement for decades. California being admitted as a free state upset this balance. To appease the south, a new federal fugitive slave law was enacted. This legislation created U.S. commissioners with incentives to recapture freedom seekers. Provisions allowed citizens to be deputized to enforce federal fugitive slave laws. The law also shifted the burden of proof to the accused black person in court proceedings. Few in congress expected the public vitriol that resulted from the legislation.

Violent confrontations broke out in many areas of Pennsylvania. Rioters attacked slave catchers outside a jail in Harrisburg for attempting to seize three freedom seekers in August 1850. In September 1851, a riot resulted in the death of a slave catcher and three black men in Lancaster. [9] During the summer of 1855, an angry mob surrounded slave catchers and rescued a runaway in Hollidaysburg. [10] The Hollidaysburg story is detailed in chapter 12 - Cumberland Valley.

The Dred Scott Decision in 1857 infuriated abolitionists and further stiffened the resolve of the anti-slavery movement. The Supreme Court ruled enslaved people were not citizens of the United States and therefore not entitled to the rights and privileges afforded to citizens from the Federal government or the courts. The opinion also stated that Congress had no authority to ban slavery in a federal territory. [11] Details of the case centered on an enslaved married couple, Dred Scott and Harriet Robinson Scott, suing for their freedom. Dred and Harriet Scott previously lived with enslavers in a free territory where slavery was prohibited but widely practiced. Bedford County has two connections to this infamous case.

Lawrence Taliaferro was the enslaver of Harriet Robinson prior to her marriage to Dred Scott. Taliaferro was born in 1794 to a prominent family in King George County, Virginia. The 1820 census report recorded 90 enslaved people living on the family estate. Lawrence enlisted in the War of 1812 and rose to the rank of 1st lieutenant. In 1818, he was granted military leave because of ill health and traveled to the mineral springs in Bedford. While recovering, he met his future wife, Eliza Dillon, the daughter of a prominent Bedford innkeeper. In 1819, Taliaferro met with President James Monroe, who encouraged him to accept a position with the Bureau of Indian Affairs. He served as an Indian agent at Fort Snelling in the Minnesota territory from 1820 to 1839.

Harriet Robinson was born in Virginia around 1820 and arrived in Fort Snelling in 1834 or 1835. Harriet was the personal servant of Eliza Dillon Taliaferro. Dred Scott and Harriet Robinson met at Fort Snelling. They were married in 1836 by Justice of the Peace, Lawrence Taliaferro. At the time of the marriage, John Emerson was the enslaver of Dred Scott. In an autobiography and on personal papers, Lawrence Taliaferro claimed he gave Harriet Robinson to Dred Scott after they married. Details of how and when Harriet Robinson Scott became enslaved to John Emerson are unclear. [12] Lawrence and Eliza Dillon Taliaferro returned to Bedford in 1839.

The second connection to Bedford was the first lawyer to represent Dred Scott and Harriet Robinson Scott. Francis B. Murdoch filed the papers for the Dred Scott v. Irene Emerson and Harriet v. Emerson lawsuits in the Circuit Court in St. Louis in 1846. Murdoch also posted a bond accepting personal responsibility for the Scott's legal costs. [13] Francis Murdoch left St. Louis prior to the Dred and Harriet Scott case going to trial. Eleven years after the filing of initial lawsuits, the Dred Scott case was appealed to the Supreme Court.

Francis Murdoch was born in Cumberland, Maryland, in 1805 and went to school at the Bedford Academy. Murdoch began practicing law in Bedford with partner Samuel M. Barclay in 1828. Samuel was the son of Hugh Barclay, a Revolutionary War veteran. Murdoch moved to the Midwest in 1831. He practiced law in Michigan and Illinois before relocating to St. Louis in 1841. Murdoch filed nearly a third of the freedom lawsuits on behalf of enslaved people in St. Louis from 1841 to 1847. He left St. Louis to practice law in San Jose, California, and later became the owner of a newspaper. Francis B. Murdock died in 1882 and is buried in the Oak Hill Memorial Park in San Jose. [14]

Early in the Civil War, Abraham Lincoln expressed a desire to issue a declaration to free enslaved people in the Confederacy. His cabinet advised against the move because the Union Army had suffered a series of battlefield defeats. Most believed it would appear to be an act of wartime desperation. Abraham Lincoln

Chapter 4 - Federal Slave Legislation 11

Images of Harriett Robinson Scott and Dred Scott. Original engraving from Frank Leslie's Illustrated Newspaper, June 27th, 1857. (Dickinson College)

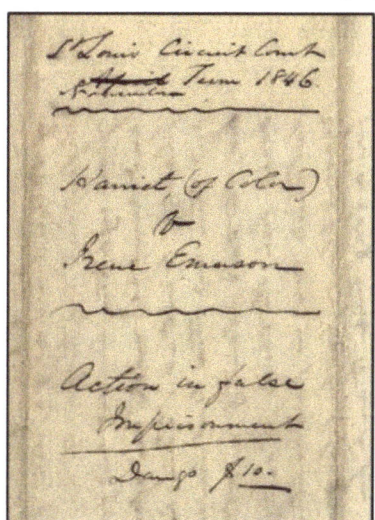

Photograph of Francis B. Murdoch in 1859 and the original handwritten note by Murdock for the Harriet v. Emerson lawsuit. (San Jose Research Library)

Eliza Dillon and Lawrence Taliaferro lived in a large house at the south-west corner of Richard and Penn Street. (Bedford County Historical Society)

made a vow to God when the Confederate Army marched toward Pennsylvania in 1862. If the invasion was turned back, he would make the declaration of freedom. [15] Lincoln pulled the previously penned Emancipation Proclamation from his desk after the battle of Antietam on September 22nd, 1862. This proclamation was only enforceable if the Union Army prevailed in the war. A steady stream of self-emancipated runaways fled toward Union Army lines during the Civil War.

The war remained deeply unpopular with Peace Democrats in the north, putting the 1864 reelection of Abraham Lincoln in doubt. Some political observers expected General George McClellan, the likely Democrat party nominee, to defeat Lincoln in the election. During a meeting in 1864, Lincoln requested black abolitionist Frederick Douglass to prepare to reconstitute the Underground Railroad. Lincoln feared McClellan would negotiate a peace settlement, leaving slavery intact. A stunned Frederick Douglass complied with the request. On September 2nd, 1864, the Union Army General William Tecumseh Sherman captured the city of Atlanta. The following month, the troops of General Philip Sheridan crushed the Rebel army in the Shenandoah Valley. These two stunning Union Army victories shifted public opinion on the war and Lincoln won re-election. [16]

On April 9th, 1865, many Bedford County soldiers in the Union Army of Ulysses S. Grant witnessed the surrender of the Confederate Army of Robert E. Lee at Appomattox. Union General Gordon Granger ordered a final enforcement of the Emancipation Proclamation on June 19th, 1865, in Galveston in Texas. The Juneteenth holiday commemorates this event as the end of slavery in America. The Thirteenth Amendment of the Constitution was enacted on December 6th, 1865, officially abolishing slavery.

Recently freed black people posing with Union soldiers in Yorktown, VA in 1862. (Library of Congress)

Chapter 5
Early Black History in Bedford County

Some of the first blacks in Bedford County came as enslaved people. In 1763, Garrett Pendergrass, a proprietor of a tavern near Fort Bedford, enslaved several people. Bedford Township tax records in 1768 show Bernard Dougherty was assessed for three enslaved people, and George Armstrong and William Rose were each accessed for one enslaved person. The 1768 Colerain Township tax records show Robert Moor was the enslaver of one person. The same year, tax records show Lewis Davison and Charles Martin were each assessed for an enslaved person in Cumberland Township. [1] A 1906 Bedford Gazette article noted both Thomas Coulter in Cumberland Valley and William Rose in Colerain Township were enslavers of one person in 1774. Courthouse records in 1780 recorded three enslaved people: 54-year-old Hercules, 30-year-old Ned, and a 17-year-old named Sam. Revolutionary War veteran Jeremiah Duvall came to the county from Ann Arundel County, MD in the 1780s. His 1786 Hopewell Township tax records listed an enslaved person. Mingo was a 20-year-old tribal chief in Africa when he was kidnapped. Duvall reportedly traded a steer for Mingo and brought him to Bedford County to tend to his horses. Mingo continued working as a hostler in the Broad Top area after gaining his freedom and lived to be 99 years old. In the 1970s, locals still referred to a spring near the cabin where he lived as Mingo's Spring. [2]

Church Revival movements in southern states resulted in some enslaved people being set free. Evangelical pastors with anti-slavery leanings spread reform messages at camp meetings during the Second Great Awakening period in the early 1800s. Some denominations eventually forced members to choose between church membership and slavery. [3] By 1860, over 250,000 free blacks were living in the south. Some recently freed enslaved people migrated to northern states. [4] The 1850 census recorded 405 free blacks living in Bedford County. By the eve of the Civil War, the black population in Bedford County had increased to 494.

Two large groups of former enslaved people came to Bedford County after being freed by benevolent enslavers in Virginia. Prior to 1849, John Dean of Romney, Virginia, freed 25 enslaved people and purchased 300 acres in Cumberland Valley for them to cultivate. Dean also provided money to live on while establishing the farmland. Unfortunately, the land was not sufficiently fertile and most eventually moved to Bedford to find work. Among this group of freed people were David, George, Jacob, and Abraham Tillman.

Prior to his death, Thomas O.B. Carter, of Fauquier County, Virginia, offered to free all enslaved people on his plantation and buy land for them in Ohio. Documents contain varying numbers, between 38 to 86 people were eventually freed. Carter apparently treated the enslaved people well. Some remained with him on his Virginia property. Carter passed away in 1840. As promised, his will freed all enslaved people and money was set aside to buy land in a northern state. Carter was a bachelor, but some potential heirs contested the will. Litigation on the will took 9 years to settle and much of his estate was squandered on lawyer fees. Some of the enslaved people from the Carter plantation purchased a large tract of land seven miles south of Bedford in 1850. Among the people who migrated to Bedford County were John Love, Jesse Slaughter, Nathan Warren, George Paynes, John Ferguson, John Alexander, and James Hollinger, Andrew Dean, Chauncey Love, Daniel Tolar, and Thomas Bruce. The land selected was also not sufficiently fertile to support the number of families in the group and eventually, most also moved to Bedford to find work. Some families later moved to Blair and Huntington Counties. [5]

Among the enslaved people from the Carter plantation was a young girl, Mary Robinson. Mary was a well-known resident of Bedford who passed away in 1938 at age 91. Mary and Preston Stewart married in 1870. Preston was born into slavery in South Carolina in 1845. It is not known how Preston gained his freedom. He was assigned by the army to accompany the body of Major William Watson Anderson of the 20th Pennsylvania Cavalry to Bedford in January 1865. Major Watson died after being thrown from his horse in Harpers Ferry, WV. Preston remained with the Anderson family for a short period before deciding to make Bedford his home. His obituary in 1910 stated, "Preston is perhaps the most widely known colored man in the county, and, though advanced in years, is still young in spirit and genial as of yore." [6]

Most enslavers were not benevolent or enlightened. Mariah Cooper was born in Virginia around 1815. Her enslaver planned to free all enslaved people on his property when he died. Prior to his passing, his greedy son took Mariah's husband to be sold. While they were gone, Mariah's white half-sister aided her escape to Bedford. She married Nelson Davis around 1840, and they had several children. One son, DeCharmes Davis, enlisted as a corporal in the 32nd U.S.C.T. in the Civil War. DeCharmes was a substitute teacher at one of the first two Bedford area schools for black children. [7]

As a young boy, George Lewis witnessed his mother and sister being sold at an auction. He escaped slavery and made his way to Bedford County from Romney, Virginia. He attended Howard University in Washington, DC and became a minister in the African Methodist Episcopal Zion Church. [8]

Another black who escaped slavery became a bishop in the A.M.E. Zion church. A book on the church published in 1895 provided a biography of Bishop John Jamison Moore. John Moore was born around 1804 in Berkeley County, Virginia. John was born free, but his family was kidnapped and enslaved. His parents, a sibling, and John escaped and came to Pennsylvania in 1820. Four of his siblings were caught during the escape and returned to slavery. Afterward, John was an indentured servant to a farmer in Bedford County. Indentured servitude for black and white people for a set number of years was not uncommon in this era. Another man, a friendly Quaker, helped John after he was no longer bound by the agreement. During his time in Bedford County, John learned to read and write. While in Harrisburg in 1833, John embraced religion. He hired private teachers to help him study English, Latin, Greek and Hebrew. John became a preacher in the A.M.E. Zion church in Philadelphia in 1839 and gained a reputation as a brilliant orator. John J. Moore was ordained as a bishop in 1868. [9]

DeCharmes Davis posing in front of the Bedford Courthouse prior to a Decoration Day (Memorial Day) event in 1918. (undated Bedford Gazette photograph – courtesy of the Bedford County Historical Society)

The Fryle and Bailey families were among a group of enslaved runaways who lived in homes on two knobs on or near Evitts Mountain. The enclave became known as "Negro Knob." [10] Limited documentation exists of runaways who assimilated in the free black communities of Bedford County. A Bedford Gazette article in 1948 listed the family names of some early black settlers: Davis, Harris, Coleman, Proctor, Wilson, Graham, Henry, and Neil. A black community near New Buena Vista included the surnames: Young, Crawley, Berry, Fry, Strong, Grey, and Burgess. This community was nearly wiped out by a small-pox epidemic in 1872. Gravestones marked with the year of the tragedy are on a hillside near where their homes once stood. [11]

Image of Bishop John Jamison Moore. (Library of Congress)

Benjamin Lyons was born into slavery. Jacob Snowberger brought Benjamin to Martinsburg from Franklin County. He was a capable young man and trusted by Snowberger to haul grain on a six-horse team wagon unaccompanied. Benjamin began transporting grain to Baltimore and Pittsburgh when he was 16 years old. Benjamin gained his freedom around 1808 on his 28th birthday, per terms in the Gradual Abolition Act of 1780. Snowberger provided the land for Benjamin to start a farm in Woodbury Township. In 1882, his son James H. Lyons became the first Salemville postmaster in South Woodbury Township. Benjamin's grandson, George W. Lyons, was a sergeant in the 41st Regiment in the U.S.C.T. during the Civil War. [12]

Henry Barks was born near Sharpsburg, MD around 1812 to a white father and black mother. He was raised as a free black child by Jacob and Anna Strohmenger, a white family in Cumberland Valley. [13] Henry was an agent in the Bedford County Underground Railroad. His son, William Tecumseh Barks, volunteered in the 54th Massachusetts, one of the first black regiments of the Civil War. The critically acclaimed 1989 motion picture "Glory" featured the 54th Massachusetts and the assault on Fort Wagner. After the war, William moved to Pittsburgh and became a prominent leader in the black community. He was also a published writer and a celebrated poet. [14] Two granddaughters of Henry Barks, Carrie and Susan Barks, joined Richard Davis as the first three blacks to graduate from Bedford High School in 1895. [15]

Photograph of the Benjamin Lyon home. (Historical Sketches of Morrisons Cove)

Some free blacks came to Bedford County from eastern Pennsylvania. In 1834, Robert and Elizabeth Wallace, their daughter Susan and her husband, William Cosler, arrived from Chambersburg. They settled near the Smith Reservoir, west of Bedford. William Cosler was a well-known wagoner in the county. Brothers Joseph and William Burgess were born near Fort Louden in Franklin County before coming to Bedford County. Both owned farms in Juniata Township. [16]

A 1906 Bedford Gazette article provided a listing of blacks in Bedford County who were born as free men and women. Mentioned were John Wilson, Moses Brown, Robert Brown, John Fiddler, Joseph Crawley, John Crawley, Henry Crawford, Israel and Nancy Martin, Edward Norris, Benjamin Gates, Reuben Gates, Richard Hamilton, Charles Harris, William Gordon, Jackson Green, Perry Brown, George Gates, Amos Harris, William Johnson and William Good. William Good was a veteran of the Mexican War in the 1840s. Many people on this list are believed to have come to Bedford County from Maryland. [17]

William Tecumseh Barks. (Undated photo on William T. Barks findagrave.com page)

George Washington Williams was born near the Bedford Springs Resort in 1849. His parents, Thomas and Ellen Rouse Williams, were both born in Pennsylvania. George ran away from home when he was 14 years old to join the Union Army. In October 1863, George volunteered in the 13th U.S.C.T. regiment under an assumed name. After the war, he became a Baptist minister, an Ohio state legislator, and one of the most important black historians of the 19th century. George wrote two trailblazing books, the "History of the Negro Race in America from 1619 to 1880" and "A History of the Negro Troops in the War of the Rebellion." He died in 1891 in Blackpool, England while returning from a trip to Africa. [18]

The 1860 county census recorded 88 black males of military age. Black regiments were first organized in 1863. Ninety-two blacks from Bedford County enlisted in the Civil War, a number higher than those available to serve three years earlier. There are several possibilities for the discrepancy. Black males of military age may have moved into the county after the 1860 census, others like George Washington Williams, may have been underage volunteers, and some recently escaped people

Mexican War Veteran Bill Good. (undated Bedford Gazette photograph – B.C.H.S.)

may have hidden from census workers. Regardless, it appears virtually every black male of military age fought in the Civil War. The following is a listing of the Bedford County soldiers and the U.S.C.T. regiments.

Name	Regiment	Name	Regiment	Name	Regiment
Allen, Henry T	43rd	Ganz, Thomas		Miller, Charles W	32nd
Barks, Alfred	41st	Gates, Reuben	3rd	Miller, David	32nd
Barks, John R	32nd	Gibson, John	2nd	Parker, James	
Barks, Moore	32nd	Gordon, Daniel	43rd	Perry, Wythe	3rd
Barks, William T	54th Mass.	Harris, John T	3rd	Plowden, Jacob	3rd
Barns, Robert	32nd	Harris, Joshua	55th Mass	Plowden, John C	3rd
Bates, Thomas	24th	Hollinger, Stephen	43rd	Reed, Louis	12th
Berry, John W	41st	Holmes, Philip	45th	Smith, Samuel	
Bolden, Elijah	6th	Johnson, David	1st	Stewart, Preston	118th
Boston, James	41st	Johnson, Moses	6th	Strathers, James	43rd
Boston, John		Johnson, William	3rd	Strathers, Willis	43rd
Brice, John	3rd	Jordon, Henry	8th	Streets, James	24th
Brown, Henry	3rd	Key, James	32nd	Streets, Rankin	
Brown, John	3rd	Key, Philip	32nd	Swartz, John	30th
Brown, Todd	3rd	Krausen, E W		Tillman, George	41st
Burk, Cory S	5th	Lewis, Bert	32nd	Tillman, Isaac	
Burk, Thomas	55th	Lewis, George T.	32nd	Tillman, Jackson	32nd
Byers, Peter		Lewis, Robert	41st	Tobias, John B	
Callahan, James	8th	Lewis, Robert M	8th	Warren, Nimrod	43rd
Carson, John	22nd	Lisles, George	3rd	Watkins, Hiram	26th & 55th
Coleman, George	32nd	Love, George		Webster, Daniel	
Costler, John		Love, John R	41st	Willard, Lewis	127th
Costler, Joseph	127th	Luckett, Alexander	32nd	Williams, Henry S	
Davis, James	24th	Lumac, William	43rd	Williams, George W	13th
Davis, John	22nd, 24th & 8th	Lyles, David	3rd	Wilson, Henry W	
Davis, DeCharmes	32nd	Lyles, George	38th	Young, Aaron	24th
Dean, Andrew		Lyles, James	3rd	Young, Daniel D	24th
Dean, Jacob	32nd	Lyons, George W	41st	Young, Jacob	127th
Doogen, Henry		Marshall, Martin	10th & 75th	Young, Jacob P	24th
Fry, Henry	43rd	McPherson, Cyrus		Young, Peter	127th
Fry, John	43rd	McPherson, John	3rd		

Five black county soldiers lost their lives in the Civil War: John Fry, Joshua Harris, Stephen Hollinger, John McPherson, and Willis Strathers. Earlier in the war, the U.S.C.T. regiments were staffed with white officers. Four white officers from Bedford County volunteered to serve in the U.S.C.T.: William Hartley, Frank Holsinger, Howard B. Jeffries, and Josiah Slick. [19]

Many blacks became property owners in the 1850s, 1860s and 1870s in Bedford County, including some women. From 1865 to 1875, three black women, Lydia Young, Catherine Gordon, Ann Elizabeth Marshall, purchased property in Bedford. Nancy Watkins, a woman who escaped slavery, bought a house in Everett. [20]

In addition to owning farms, blacks started businesses. Aaron and Jacob Young were proprietors of a butcher shop in Bedford that provided much of the meat for the town. Most of the barber shops in Bedford and Everett were owned by black men. [21] Bruce Fisher Photography was owned by two black men in Everett. Blacks worked as blacksmiths, tanners, coopers, chefs, and shoemakers in the county. At the turn of the century, Edward and Alberta Harris built and operated the Harris Hotel. Howard and Elizabeth Harris owned a restaurant in the Greystone Hotel. [22]

Thriving 19th century black communities in Bedford County is an inspiring story. From humble beginnings, much was achieved. Many blacks owned their homes and had started businesses. Black churches were founded in Bedford and Everett. County blacks become college graduates, clergy, teachers, published authors, elected officials, and lawyers. Ninety-two black citizens served in the Union Army during the Civil War. [23]

Well-known community leader William P. Schell shared some observations in a Bedford Gazette article in 1906. Schell was a former Speaker of the Pennsylvania House of Representatives and a former member of the State Senate. Schell wrote black people in Bedford County had been good citizens during the previous century. Stating they were industrious, frugal, honest, religious, and liked by white people. [24]

George Washington Williams in 1891.
(Library of Congress)

Copperheads Cartoon published in Harper's Weekly - February 1863. (Library of Congress)

Chapter 6
A Divisive Time

The political environment prior to and during the Civil War was often toxic and ugly. At opposite ends of the spectrum were the abolitionists and the supporters of slavery. Both had been exchanging increasingly bitter words for decades. In the years leading up to the Civil War, violent actions between the two groups became more common. Some citizens were indifferent to both.

William Maclay Hall was a retired judge in Bedford and a noted advocate of blacks in the county. Hall was the grantor on several property deed transactions with blacks in the years following the Civil War. [1] He authored, Reminiscences and Sketches, Historical and Biographical, in 1890. The following is an excerpt from a short-story in the book, Slave Catching in Bedford County.

> The slave-hunters of Bedford County, the men who received and posted the handbills and got the rewards, were looked down upon and despised by their neighbors. The name of slave-catcher was nearly as much a stigma as the name of abolitionist. The public sentiment of the better class of the community condemned both with an equal measure of contempt. [2]

Prior to and during the Civil War, pitched battles periodically ensued between the Bedford Gazette and the Bedford Inquirer. The two newspapers sat on opposite sides of the political divide. On January 2nd, 1857, David Over, publisher of the Bedford Inquirer, responded to a recent article in the Bedford Gazette. The following is an excerpt.

> In our paper of the 19th December, we took occasion to refer to the unmitigated falsehood of the Gazette. In the last issue of the paper, (the Gazette) sticks to the late campaign, that the (anti-slavery) opposition "boldly avowed that a Negro was better than a white man." It is a compound of absurdity and folly, malignity, and baseness, leaving the reader in great doubt whether the proper place for its author would be the lunatic asylum, or the State penitentiary. [3]

When the Civil War erupted in 1861, newspapers reflected the deep divisions that existed in Bedford County. The Inquirer agreed with Lincoln on crushing the rebellion by force if necessary. The Gazette blamed the war on abolitionists not being willing to make accommodations on slavery with the South. On April 26th, 1861, the Gazette announced the surrender of Fort Sumter. The following are excerpts from the article titled "Old Abe's War".

> ABRAHAM LINCOLN, the poor imbecile who occupies and disgraces the Presidential chair, has thought proper to commence a civil war—and what a commencement. The first battle is a triumph for South Carolina! Fort Sumter has surrendered to the enemy, and the great North and her people stand defeated and disgraced before the world! The extreme Abolitionists, who direct and control LINCOLN, were the men who demanded a civil war. Blood has been spilled - men have been shot down by their brethren. When hostilities are to cease, God only knows. We may in all probability will have a war of years, and our country may be drenched with blood before the end. Our Union is doomed - doomed because of the triumph of an unprincipled sectional Abolition party. Heaven protect us! [4]

Excerpt of a Bedford Gazette article published on April 26th, 1861. (Newspapers.com)

This article was prophetic. The war would indeed last years, and many local men and boys would fall on bloody killing fields and perish in disease infested camps during the Civil War.

A few years earlier, Abraham Lincoln was a little-known state legislator in Illinois. After securing the Republican nomination for the U.S. Senate in 1858, Lincoln delivered the well-remembered "a house divided against itself cannot stand" speech. Most were familiar with the phrasing. Jesus made a similar statement in the gospels. Democrat nominee Stephen Douglas and Lincoln faced off in a series of famous debates over slavery. Lincoln lost the 1858 election. But the debates with Douglas led to Lincoln being swept into the White House two years later. Lincoln's election triggered the secession of southern states and the beginning of the Civil War. [5]

A man from St. Clair Township wrote a letter to the editor in the Bedford Gazette on May 24th, 1861. The letter was a response to an article published in the Bedford Inquirer. The writer expressed the following sentiments.

> We love peace, we can see no good in war. Our homes are happier, our firesides brighter, when no enemy lurks around. We would prefer letting slavery alone, mind our own business, and let slavery take care of itself. If a sin, we are not responsible for it. If no sin, then we have committed a very grave sin by meddling ourselves with it, and bringing about, or at least helping to bring about, this inglorious fight of Cain with Abel. [6]

A nasty salvo from one newspaper editor often triggered an even nastier volley in response. At times, every insult imaginable was hurled that could have been uttered in polite company. The following is an excerpt from an article published in the Bedford Gazette on August 16th, 1861. The title of the article is "WHO ARE THE REAL TRAITORS?"

> The Inquirer clique, the malignant and villainous slanderers of better men and truer patriots than themselves, still persist in their charges of treason against quiet, law-abiding and peaceable citizens of Bedford. These fellows composing that clique, are the most miserable of liars and the cowardliest of poltroons, at the same time they are the vilest of blackguards and the guiltiest of TRAITORS. They are the falsest hypocrites, the meanest dirt-eaters, the lowest demagogues, the filthiest buzzards that ever pretended to honesty, friendship or patriotism, or that ever gorged their greedy maws at the public crib. They were always dastard and contemptible, pharisaic, deceitful, and treacherous, unprincipled, unscrupulous, and ungentlemanly, cowardly, mean, and low, but since that pestiferous insect, the Treason-smeller, has got under their clothes, every devilish drop in their veins has become more Satanic, every hellish wish in their hearts more infernal, every dark and deadly thought of their minds, tenfold blacker and deadlier. Such monsters need exposition. The people MUST KNOW what these devils incarnate are afraid they will learn, viz: That they themselves, the howling, whining, whimpering BLACK REPUBLICAN EDITORS, ARE THE TRAITORS! That THEY ARE THE DISUMONISTS whose deliberate treachery helped to sap the Union of its foundations. [7]

Two considerations to help quantify local sentiments are the 1860 presidential election results and the number of Union Army volunteers. Abraham Lincoln carried Bedford County in the 1860

Excerpt of Bedford Gazette article on August 16th, 1861. (Newspapers.com)

election by a margin of 2506 votes to 2324 for Democrat John Breckinridge. Two third-party candidates garnered an additional 100 votes. Out of 21 boroughs and townships in Bedford County, Lincoln carried twelve and the Democrat candidate carried nine. Twelve townships were won by significant margins by either Lincoln or Breckenridge. [8]

In March 1863, Congress enacted the first federal military draft in American history. Prior to this draft, 2,228 men and boys from Bedford County enlisted as volunteers, roughly two-thirds of white men of military age volunteered during the first two years of the war. After March 1863, it is not possible to determine the total numbers of volunteers vs. draftees. Black regiments were first organized in the Union Army in 1863. Ninety-two blacks from Bedford County enlisted in the Union Army. The 1860 county census listed only 88 black males between the ages of 20 and 49. It appears virtually every black male of military age in Bedford County enlisted in the Civil War. [9]

Copperheads was a derogatory term used to describe Peace Democrats who were against the war. Lincoln supporters often suspected some Peace Democrats were secretly sympathetic to the south and slavery. At odds with this narrative is the story of George W. Gump. Gump lived in Napier Township and was a Democrat party nominee for the state legislature in 1859. The 1850 census listed Gump as being a previous resident of Cumberland, Maryland. In 1861, Gump received an anonymous letter accusing him of attending a secessionist meeting in Cumberland, MD. Gump vigorously denied the allegation in a letter to the Gazette published on May 31st, 1861. He even offered a $500 reward to anyone who could prove the allegation. Three years later, his son, Lt. John A. Gump of the 138th PA Infantry, died from wounds received during the battle of Cedar Creek. The following are some excerpts of a moving article published in the Bedford Gazette on November 25th, 1864.

DISTRICTS.	Dem. Electors.	Douglas Electors.	Bell Electors.	Lincoln Electors.
Bedford Bor.,	106	7	15	107
Bedford tp.	214	6	6	143
Broad Top.	28	1	4	72
Cumb. Valley	186		1	19
Colerain	124			102
Harrison	57		19	61
Hopewell	54		3	116
Juniata	155		3	96
Londonderry	77		3	73
Liberty	80		2	73
Monroe	103			180
Napier	170		3	149
Prov. E.	49		2	171
Prov. W.	50		2	177
Schellsburg	48		2	31
Snake Spring	56		4	71
Southampton	175			62
St. Clair	137		16	248
Union	135		1	184
Woodberry M.	113			235
Woodberry S.	107			135
Totals	2324	14	86	2506

Bedford Gazette article on November 16th, 1860 on Presidential election results by Boro and Township. (Newspapers.com)

George W. and Sophia Stuckey Gump. (The Gump Family in America)

> It is needless to dwell upon the many ennobling traits of character possessed by this lamented youth. We knew John Gump as a boy of quick perception, steady habits and manly bearing; and we believe, "None knew him but to love him, None named him but to praise." The following is taken from a letter of Capt. J. T. Rorer, of the 138th, to the father of the deceased, written from Winchester, Va., on the 23rd. The Lieutenant has, during the whole of the campaign, been my constant companion on the staff of our brigade. My affection for him is as a brother. He was a true and steadfast friend—a brave and courageous soldier. He was, indeed, among the most active of officers and his place cannot be refilled from our brigade. We might continue the testimony to the worth and gallantry of the noble lieutenant, but it is unnecessary. His memory will be gratefully cherished by many mourning friends and when the sod shall grow green above his resting place, his name will be recalled with pleasure by associates and admirers, as that of one who was every inch a man. [10]

After the battle of Antietam in 1862, Lincoln issued the Emancipation Proclamation, freeing all enslaved people in the Confederacy - if the Union Army prevailed in the war. This action clarified what was at stake in the Civil War.

By election day in November 1864, nearly 500 Bedford County men and boys had perished in the war. Lincoln was running against democrat George McClellan, the former commander of the Union Army. Two years earlier, McClellan was dismissed by Lincoln for failing to prosecute the war aggressively. If McClellan won, peace negotiations with the Confederacy were expected, leaving open the possibility of slavery continuing in the south.

The final 1864 presidential elections totals in Bedford County are not known. These results did not include over 2,000 Bedford County soldiers who had to vote remotely from the war front. The preliminary results in Bedford County were 2585 votes for McClellan and 1954 votes for Lincoln. An estimated 78 percent of all Union soldiers cast their votes for Lincoln in the election. If the votes of soldiers were included, Lincoln would have easily carried Bedford County a second time. A soldier in the 208th PA Infantry sent a letter to the Inquirer with voting results of Bedford County soldiers in the regiment. Lincoln received 111 votes to 35 for McClellan. Lincoln won the 1864 election in a landslide. McClellan carried only the border states of Kentucky and Delaware, and his home state of New Jersey. [11]

Reluctance or opposition to wars has been a common occurrence in American history. Many people living today have vivid recollections of the deep divisions during the Vietnam War. Differing viewpoints on entering wars stretch back to the founding of America. Many American colonists remained loyal to the British in the Revolutionary War. William Franklin, governor of New Jersey and son of Benjamin Franklin, was a loyalist who was exiled to England during the war. Isolationist sentiments initially kept the United States out of both world wars in the 20th century. The First World War raged in Europe for nearly 3 years before America declared war on Germany in April 1917. [12] The German invasion of Poland in September 1939 triggered the start of Second World War. America remained out of this war for two years. Only after the surprise attack on Pearl Harbor on December 7th, 1941, did a shocked and enraged Congress declare war on Japan. Four days after Pearl Harbor, it was Adolf Hitler who declared war on the United States, not the other way around.

Regardless of the differing political viewpoints, more Bedford County men and boys lost their lives in a war that was fundamentally fought over slavery than in all other wars in American history combined.

Chapter 7
Geography and Transportation

Geography and transportation were key factors in the flow of freedom seekers into Bedford County. Two slave states were in close proximity. Bedford County shares a border with Maryland and Virginia was less than 10 miles away. Before the Civil War, the Potomac River separated Maryland from Virginia. Slightly more than half of the 171,131 blacks in Maryland and nearly 90 percent of the 548,907 blacks in Virginia were enslaved. [1]

Cumberland, Maryland, was a major transportation hub in the decades leading up to the Civil War. The first federally funded road in American history ran through Cumberland. Route 40, referred to then as the National Road or the Baltimore Pike, connected Baltimore with the Ohio River in 1834. The Baltimore & Ohio rail-line extended to Cumberland in 1842. The Chesapeake & Ohio Canal was completed in 1850, linking Cumberland to Washington, D.C. [2] Enslaved people worked on the National Road, the B & O railroad, and the C & O Canal during construction. After completion, they worked transporting goods. Familiarity with these routes led to more freedom seekers crossing the nearby Pennsylvania border.

The National Road skirted the Bedford County border and was heavily traveled from daylight through the early evening hours. The two most common vehicles on the road were stagecoaches and Conestoga wagons. People could travel 60 to 70 miles a day on stagecoaches. Six-horse Conestoga wagons carrying agricultural and manufactured goods traveled about 15 miles per day. Taverns, blacksmith shops and livery stables sprang up in small towns and villages along the route. [3] By the mid-1840s, the transportation business on the National Road was booming, and Cumberland had become a bustling center of commerce. Enslaved people traveling on the National Road was a common sight. [4] The following is an excerpt from a book published on the road in 1894.

> Negro slaves were frequently seen on the National Road. The writer has seen them driven over the road arranged in couples and fastened to a long, thick rope or cable, like horses. This may seem incredible to a majority of persons now living along the road, but it is true, and was a very common sight in the early history of the road and evoked no expression of surprise or words of censure. Such was the temper of the times. There were also negro waggoners on the road, but negro stage drivers were unknown. [5]

Turn of the 20th century photograph of the National Road (route 40) west of Cumberland, Maryland. (Western Maryland Historical Library)

A six-horse team pulling a Conestoga wagon at an unknown location. (Library of Congress)

The Maryland State Archives contains information of an attempted stagecoach escape near Cumberland. James Harris was a 56-year-old black farmer in Allegany County. He was born into slavery but had gained his freedom. His family members were still enslaved. On August 13th, 1863, James hailed a stagecoach carrying his wife and daughters near the Flintstone Hotel, 10 miles east of Cumberland. He paid the stagecoach fares and arranged for a room at the next station, five miles from Cumberland. James was overheard instructing family members to remain there until their departure for Uniontown, PA, the next evening. James was arrested and sentenced to six years and six months in the Maryland Penitentiary on October 15th, 1863. The eleven jurors who heard the case and five members of the state legislature petitioned the governor to pardon James Harris. The following year, the state of Maryland abolished slavery. The governor pardoned James Harris on December 20th, 1864. [6]

Turn of the 20th century photograph of the Flintstone Hotel along the National Road (route 40) east of Cumberland, Maryland. (Western Maryland Historical Library.)

Chapter 7 - Geography and Transportation   25

Baltimore and Ohio Railroad circa June 1859, crossing the Bollman truss bridge that spanned the Potomac River, east of Cumberland, Maryland. (Maryland Center for History and Culture)

The Baltimore and Ohio Railroad line reached Cumberland in 1842. Before the western extension of the rail-line in the early 1850s, passengers and cargo were unloaded at Cumberland and transported west via the National Road. The B&O museum at the historic Mt. Clare Station in Baltimore features a permanent exhibit on the Underground Railroad. The museum features the lives and journeys of 27 freedom seekers who traveled on the railroad. Some donned elaborate disguises. Ellen Craft, who was light-skinned, posed as a sickly white male enslaver while her husband William, posed as a faithful servant. After their successful escape in 1848, the Crafts fled to England after the 1850 Fugitive Slave Act passed. [7]

Etching of Ellen and William Craft. (The Underground Railroad Museum at Mt. Clare, MD)

The Chesapeake & Ohio Canal transported coal, lumber, and agricultural goods along a 184-mile towpath. Completing construction of the canal connecting Washington, D.C. and Cumberland was a remarkable engineering feat in 1850. The project required 74 locks, 7 dams, 11 aqueducts, and a 3,118-foot tunnel. A C&O Canal newsletter published a study on the labor of enslaved people on the canal and an examination of newspaper ads mentioning the canal and escapes. [8] During construction, workers were housed in remote locations, affording opportunities to disappear into heavily wooded areas near the border of Pennsylvania.

A horse pulling a Chesapeake & Ohio Canal boat. (Western Maryland Historical Library)

After construction, blacks working on towboats became familiar with the city of Cumberland. Connections were made with city residents willing to help enslaved people. The biography of Reverend Hillhouse Buel mentioned runaways followed the canal to Cumberland, Maryland, hiding in thick bushes and waiting for a signal to proceed to an Underground Railroad station. [9]

An interesting newspaper article published in 1900 reported two skeletons found chained together in a cave on Round Top hill. Round Top hill is approximately 4 miles southwest of Hancock, near the C & O Canal. Found near the skeletons were a silver dollar and a half dollar, coined in 1840 and 1847. Whether the skeletons were of enslaved people or slave catchers is not known. [10]

From safe houses in Cumberland, Maryland, many freedom seekers took one of two routes through Bedford County. One routing ran through Cumberland Valley Township, between the ridges of Wills Mountain and Evitts Mountain. A second cited routing ran east of Evitts Mountain, toward the village of Chaneysville. Some freedom seekers traveled on or near ancient Indian paths. These paths, along rugged mountain terrain and wooded rolling hills, helped runaways avoid detection. [11] The Pennsylvania Historical and Museum Commission sponsored a study in 1965 of Indian paths in the state. Three paths from the Potomac River near Cumberland run in a northeastern direction through Pennsylvania. These paths are referred to as the "Warriors Paths."

One Warriors Path runs from Old Town, Maryland crosses the state line at Flintstone and proceeds east of Chaneysville. The path continues along Black Valley to Bloody Run (Everett).

A second Warriors Path runs from Cresaptown, Maryland passes to the west of Cumberland and crosses the state line at Ellerslie. This path continues past Hyndman, skirts the west side of Wills Mountain, and proceeds to Manns Choice a few miles west of Bedford.

A third Warriors Path runs from the mouth of Wills Creek in Cumberland, Maryland and crosses the Pennsylvania line at Shriver Ridge gap. The path weaves through Cumberland Valley Township between Wills and Evitts Mountain. It proceeds past Centerville to a point near Burning Bush, eight miles south of Bedford. The trail direction from Burning Bush has been debated. The path may have veered toward the Bedford Springs Hotel and skirted the eastern side of Bedford. Another possibility is the path proceeded toward the western side of Bedford. [12]

Enslaved people in central and western Virginia were aware of the Appalachian Mountain range pointed northward. Some runaways navigated the hills and mountains of Bedford County without the help of the

Chapter 7 - Geography and Transportation 27

Underground Railroad. They were unaware of those sympathetic to their plight. Some traveled at night, others proceeded cautiously during the day. Some walked along main roads, others took less traveled paths on northward pointing ridges. Freedom seekers could have crossed into Bedford County anywhere along the approximate 25-mile-long border with Maryland. Routes taken through the county would have depended on where the border was crossed.

My ancestors have lived on property along Rays Hill Mountain since before the Civil War. While growing up, my grandmother always referred to a path that ran along Rays Hill as the Negro Road. One day I asked about the origins of the name. She didn't know. This was the name always cited for as long as she could remember. She mentioned previous generations rarely talked about the past. My grandmother was born in 1913 and was two generations removed from those who would have known the origins of the name. Rays Hill runs in a northeastern direction toward Huntingdon County. Prior to the Civil War, black people lived in areas known as "Black Log Valley" or "Black Valley" in Huntingdon County.[13] Black communities in Huntingdon County exist today. Another Black Valley is in Bedford County between Chaneysville and Everett. Folklore on the origins of the name Black Valley, is covered in chapter 11 - Bloody Run and Rainsburg.

The Warriors Path marker in Flintstone, Maryland.

"Negro Road" path on Rays Hill.

Cumberland, Maryland Area Map

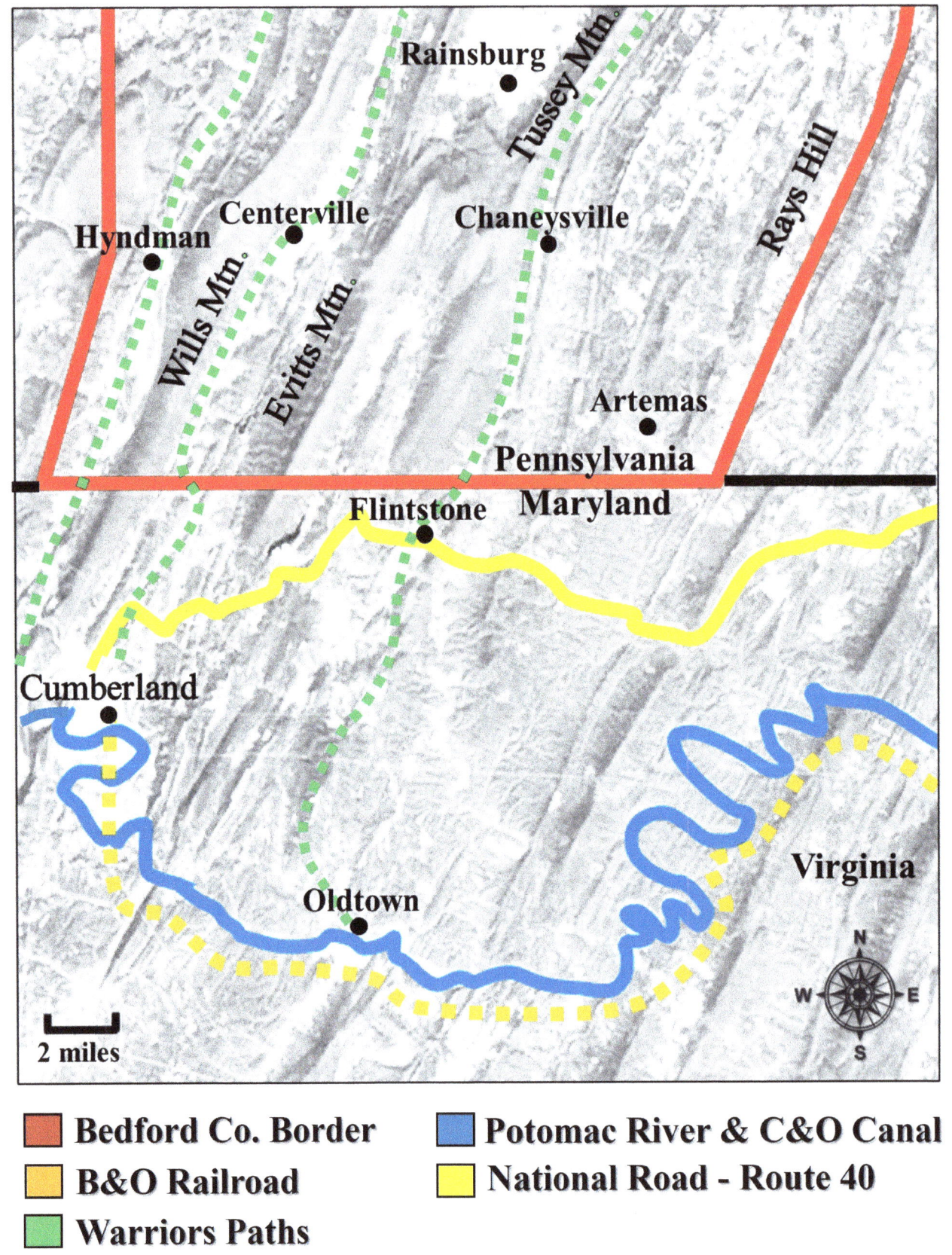

Chapter 8
North Star

Any trek to freedom was fraught with peril and apprehension. All that was familiar was cast aside. Family and friends were left behind. An uncertain future loomed in an unknown world. Unsure were the distances to be traveled or dangers to be faced. A significant but unknown number of enslaved people began their journey without the help of the Underground Railroad. Many desperate escape attempts were made, with the North Star serving as the only guide.

It is difficult to overstate the importance of the North Star as a beacon of freedom. Black abolitionist Frederick Douglass symbolically named his anti-slavery newspaper the "North Star". [1] Enslaved people rarely had access to maps or compass. The North Star maintains a relatively fixed position in the sky above the North Pole and had long been used for night navigation. This was widely known to enslaved people. The North Star is often located by first identifying the Big Dipper constellation. The Big Dipper was also referred to as the Drinking Gourd. [2] Follow the Drinking Gourd was a popular folk song during the Civil Rights movement and has been recorded over 200 times. First published in 1928, the verifiable origins of the song remain elusive. Some believe versions of the song date to the Underground Railroad era. [3] Traveling at night often provided the best chance to remain undetected. When clouds obscured the stars, homespun knowledge such as moss growing on the north-side of trees provided guidance. [4]

The circumstances and experiences were different for each freedom seeker. The following story, written by an enslaved person raised in Loudon County, Virginia, was published prior to the Civil War. At fifteen, Peyton Lucas became an apprentice at a blacksmith shop. Later, Peyton was hired out as a journeyman blacksmith and had many privileges. One day in 1841, the enslaver and another man came to the shop where Peyton worked. Later that day, the enslaver was overheard discussing selling Peyton for fifteen hundred dollars. A week later, Peyton and two companions fled north. After crossing the Potomac River, they traveled at night, concealed themselves during daylight for ten days. During the journey, they were tracked by dogs, narrowly avoiding capture. They suffered from hunger and exposure to rain. Periodically, people were heard working near them, but they did not dare ask for food. For three days, green corn was the only food source. One night, they broke into a farm springhouse for some much-needed milk before hurrying off when dogs began barking. The following is a verbatim excerpt of what Peyton wrote on making contact with an unknown person.

> One morning between two and four o'clock, we came to a white man tending a lime-kiln. He was asleep. We knew nothing of the way; so we concluded to awaken him, and ask the way, and if he tried to stop us, or have us caught, we would kill him and throw him into the kiln. We awoke him and told him that our harvesting was done, and we were hunting for work, as we had two days to work in. He did not believe it, - said we were runaways. I took out my pistol, cocked and capped it, and the others produced a bayonet and a bowie knife. The man approached us, saying still we were runaways. Had he offered to touch us, we would have killed him, but he proved to be the best friend we ever had. He told us the way and regretted he had no food. Said, "If you travel on, by daylight you will cross Mason and Dixon's line, and get among the Dutch. Keep away from the big road, walk near it, but not in it, - walk in the daytime, but keep in the woods." We followed his directions, and at ten o'clock the next morning, we reached a Dutchman's house.

> The man was out, - but the woman and girls set the table. We ate all they had in the house, - I ate till I was ashamed. The good woman told us to avoid Shippensburg. Six runaways had just been carried back from there. She told us, if anybody questioned us, to say we were go-

ing to the Horse Shoe Bottom camp meeting on the Susquehanna. We did accordingly, and soon stuck the track of the underground railroad, which we followed into the northern free states.

At an undisclosed location, I went to work on a building. One day a druggist came to me and said an advertisement describing me was in the tavern offering a reward of five hundred dollars. My friends advised me to remove further. I worked in Geneva, N. Y., until the passage of the fugitive slave law, when my friends advised me to go to Canada, with which advice I complied. I feel that I am out of the lion's paw, and I feel that there is no curse of god's earth equal to slavery. [5]

Peyton Lucas, being hired out by a cash strapped enslaver, was not an unusual occurrence. Estimates are 31 percent of enslaved people in urban areas and 6 percent in rural areas were hired out in the upper south. Research indicates most runaways entering Pennsylvania had been hired out during their lifetime. Hired out enslaved people could often keep a portion of their earnings, explaining how some runaways purchased food and transportation. [6]

This story cites the recommendation to "get among the Dutch." The term Dutch or Pennsylvania Dutch refers to people of German heritage. They were known to be sympathetic to enslaved people. Harriet Brumbaugh Gates grew up on a farm in Morrisons Cove just north of the Bedford County line. The area has many Dutch people. She recalled the following from the 1850s in a story published in the Morrisons Cove Herald.

One evening, as the family was enjoying a moment of relaxation following the cares of the day, a rap came at the door. Mother opens it and there stood a black man with an ax on his shoulder. Behind him stood another black man with a gun on his shoulder. Somewhat to the rear of these formidable figures were three black women, together with four children. Harriet clung to her mother's skirt. However, the fugitives from the south were merely asking for food and lodging for the night. Gathering up carpets and blankets, Mr. and Mrs. Brumbaugh built a fire in the big fireplace in the basement, fed the strangers, who afterward rolled themselves in the bedding and slept around on the floor before the fire. The poor wanderers in an alien land found sympathy and succor under the George W. Brumbaugh roof that knew no bounds of race or color. [7]

Once the Mason Dixon line was crossed, more chances were likely taken on contacting locals. Some free black and white people who were not part of the Underground Railroad provided spontaneous aid. Simple gestures, such as food, paid for or given, and directions were helpful to runaways. Those who could provide contacts associated with the Underground Railroad were very helpful.

George W. & Elizabeth Brumbaugh.
(Ellis Snare)

Harriet Brumbaugh Gates.
(Keith Gates)

Chapter 9
Cumberland Maryland

The path to freedom for many passed through the transportation hub of Cumberland, Maryland. Two churches were at the center of the Underground Railroad activity. Tunnels used by freedom seekers beneath one church can still be viewed today. The name of a circuit-riding preacher of the other church was discovered in John Brown's papers after the ill-fated Harpers Ferry raid. The Emmanuel Parish of the Episcopal and the African Methodist Episcopal churches helped many enslaved runaways who entered Bedford County.

Fort Cumberland was built in the 1750s during the French and Indian War. It sat on a prominent hill 400 yards above the Potomac River. Beneath the fort, underground chambers stored food and gunpowder. Tunnels extended beyond the walls of the fortress to the British defenses on the banks of the Potomac River and Will's Creek. By 1814, the Fort had fallen into disrepair and the land was sold to a combined Episcopal and Presbyterian congregation. The first Emmanuel Parish church building was completed in 1829. Reverend David Hillhouse Buel was appointed rector of the church in 1847. Prior to this appointment, Buel had already been active in the Underground Railroad in other parts of Maryland.

The congregation outgrew the original structure, and the construction of a new church began in 1849. An enslaver, Samuel Semmes, offered to pay 30% of construction costs of the church if a balcony was added so enslaved people could attend services. Congregation documents show a balcony for enslaved people had been added when the church was consecrated in 1851.
[1] Church records show free and enslaved black attendance grew steadily during the 1850s.

Rev. David H. Buel. (Emmanuel Parish collection)

Photograph of Baltimore Street in Cumberland in 1858. The Emmanuel Parish Episcopal church is visible on the upper right side of the picture. (Deb Lottes)

Emmanuel Parish of the Episcopal Church.

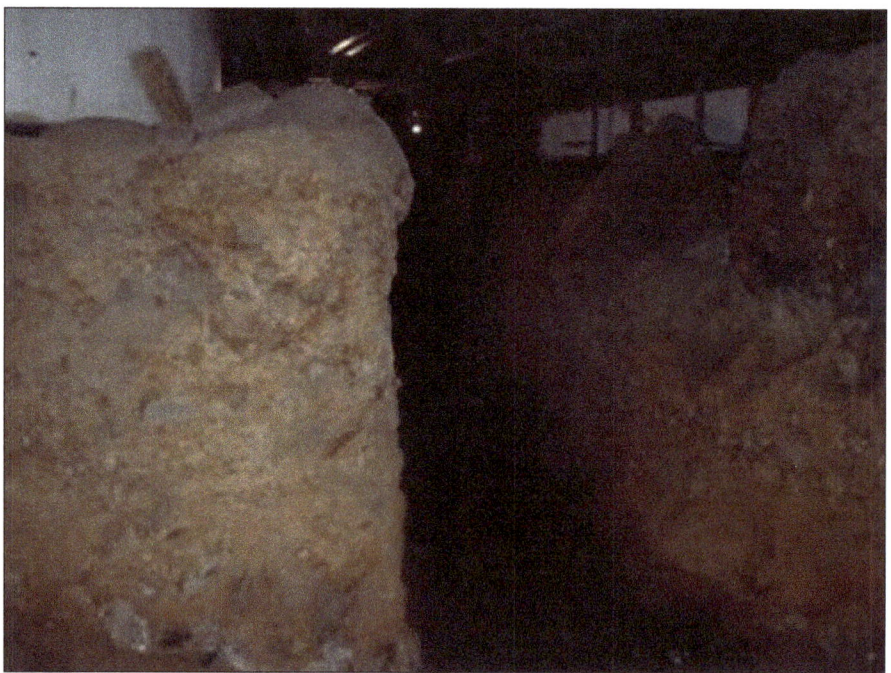
*The Tunnels beneath the Emmanuel Parish of the Episcopal Church.
(Emmanuel Parish collection)*

At the bottom of the hill, below the church, enslaved runaways hid in the Shanty Town area in Cumberland near the C & O canal. Many free blacks lived in this poor section of town. When the church bell rang in a coded way, enslaved people passed through an iron gate and proceeded in tunnels to safety beneath the church. Most rested while receiving aid, food, and instructions for the next step in their journey. When judged safe to continue, they exited out the rectory cellar door and proceeded through an unpopulated area of town toward the Mason-Dixon line. [2]

Thomas W. Henry was a circuit-riding African Methodist Episcopal preacher who was born into slavery on a large tobacco plantation in Leonardtown, MD in 1794. The plantation enslaver died in 1804. His will freed all enslaved people except those older than 54. Maryland law prohibited older enslaved people from being set free. Many over the age 54 were sold, including Thomas Henry's father. The state law also bound younger enslaved people until age 22. Thomas did not gain freedom until 1816.

At age 19, Thomas worked as a blacksmith apprentice in Hagerstown, Maryland. Soon after, Thomas attended a camp meeting across the Potomac River in Virginia and experienced a religious conversion. He began encouraging friends and acquaintances to seek the salvation of their souls. [3] Over the next twenty years, Thomas served as a lay preacher.

Thomas married his first wife, Catherine, in 1821, while she was still enslaved. Thomas made an agreement with the enslaver to purchase freedom for his wife and four children in 1827. After Thomas finished making payments for his wife and two youngest children, the enslaver raised the price of freedom for the two older children. Before Thomas could raise the money, both children were sold. [4]

Reverend Thomas Henry was ordained as a full-time preacher in 1838 and rode the Washington and Frederick County circuit for the next 7 years. The official title was traveling clergy, but the position was commonly referred to as a circuit rider or saddlebag preacher. Circuit riders preached throughout the week at any available place, including cabins, fields, and meeting houses. Sermons, baptisms, weddings, funerals, and other religious rites were provided during stops. Some rural circuits took up to six weeks to cover. [5]

In 1845, Thomas was transferred to the Chambersburg and Carlisle Circuit. This assignment began a long association with A.M.E. churches in both Maryland and Pennsylvania. His circuit responsibilities included churches in Hollidaysburg, PA and Cumberland, MD, during the next 15 years. [6] Thomas Henry's autobiography mentioned being a guest preacher at a mixed congregation church in Cumberland. It is quite possible the unnamed church was the Emmanuel Parish Episcopal. Thomas had a family connection in Cumberland. His cousin, James Henry, was a resident and a member of the Cumberland A.M.E. church. [7] Circuit riders were in a unique position to communicate with vast numbers of people to coordinate help for enslaved people seeking freedom.

On October 16th, 1859, radical abolitionist John Brown launched a raid on the government arsenal at Harpers Ferry with plans to arm enslaved people and instigate a revolt. Thomas Henry's name was found on John Brown's papers at the rented farmhouse where the raid was launched. A month later, Thomas was visiting his son in Baltimore when a newspaper article listed him as an accomplice of Brown. Thomas immediately fled Baltimore and narrowly missed being arrested. Police knocked on the door where Henry was staying 10 minutes after he boarded a train to Philadelphia. Thomas Henry was reassigned to a new A.M.E. circuit in Oswego, New York, in December 1859. [8]

Undated photograph in Cumberland. The sign on the wagon is "The Cumberland Baggage Delivery Transfer." (Allegany Museum Collection)

The years leading up to the Civil War were uneasy and uncomfortable for many in Bedford County. The institution of slavery and the return of runaways who fled into Pennsylvania had been contentious issues for decades. Safety concerns and mistrust between the citizens of Bedford County and Cumberland Maryland came to a head when the Civil War erupted in the spring of 1861. The same week the surrender of Fort Sumter was reported, a warning was published in the Bedford Gazette.

> A word to our Southern Neighbors. The latest reports by Telegraph bring us the intelligence of skirmishes and battles in Maryland, and of an intended descent upon the border villages in Pennsylvania. We would say to our neighbors, bethink yourselves of the past. The people of the border counties in Pennsylvania have always fought valiantly for your rights and yielded not till the last foothold slipped from under them. Repay not their kind offices with such ingratitude. Should you attempt to do so, former friend and former foe will be compelled to unite for the purpose of repelling your assaults. Let us have no guerilla warfare like this. [9]

The following reply from the Mayor of Cumberland was published in the Bedford Gazette on May 10th, 1861.

> Whereas, It is rumored that the peaceful relations which have heretofore existed between the citizens of Maryland and their neighbors of Pennsylvania have been broken up by the unfortunate condition of national affairs, and that intercourse is dangerous to Pennsylvanians, and a multitude of wild and unfounded rumors are, as we are informed, in circulation, calculated to create distrust and unfriendly feelings on the part of our neighbors in Bedford and Somerset Counties against the citizens of Cumberland and Allegany county. Therefore, be it resolved, That the Mayor give notice by handbill and otherwise that Maryland is yet a portion of the United States, and that we profess no less loyalty to the Constitution, no less friendship to our neighbors of Pennsylvania than we have heretofore done, and that we apprehend no danger from them and assure them they need fear none from us. [10]

On the same page as this reply from the mayor of Cumberland, another article wrote of steps being taken to protect Bedford County.

> Efforts are now being made to have a camp of volunteers at Bedford. We consider this a very important point. Maryland is loyal, and Cumberland, which is but thirty miles from here, has only the Potomac River between it and Virginia. Cumberland is overwhelmingly for the Union, but it is a large town, and an important point, and has already been threatened by the traitors. It may be of the utmost importance for this part of Pennsylvania and Maryland, that there should be a regiment, at least, of troops at this place. [11]

Though some residents joined the Confederate Army, the state of Maryland remained loyal to the United States during the war. In 1863, West Virginia split away from Virginia over slavery. Confederate cavalry units conducted guerrilla warfare in Western Maryland, West Virginia, and Pennsylvania during the Civil War. In July 1864, around 2,800 Confederate cavalry soldiers of General John McCausland entered Chambersburg and demanded a ransom which was not met. After burning Chambersburg, the Confederate path of destruction veered west toward Bedford County. The cavalry of Union General William Averell caught up with the raiders near McConnellsburg and forced a retreat toward Hancock. After crossing the Maryland border, the Rebels proceeded on the National Road toward Cumberland Maryland. The B&O Rail facilities were a likely target. Two Union army regiments of approximately 1000 men set up a defensive line east of Cumberland. On August 1st, 1864, the battle of Folck's Mill occurred near the intersection of present-day Route 220 and Route 68. The Rebel force retreated south after clashing with Union infantry in their front and Union cavalry approaching their rear. The Union cavalry relentlessly chased the rebel raiders and exacted revenge during the Battle of Moorefield on August 7th. That fall, Union Cavalry units burned wide swaths of farmland in the Shenandoah Valley near Winchester. Bedford County luckily avoided the type of destruction suffered by other nearby areas during the Civil War.

Bedford County Area Map

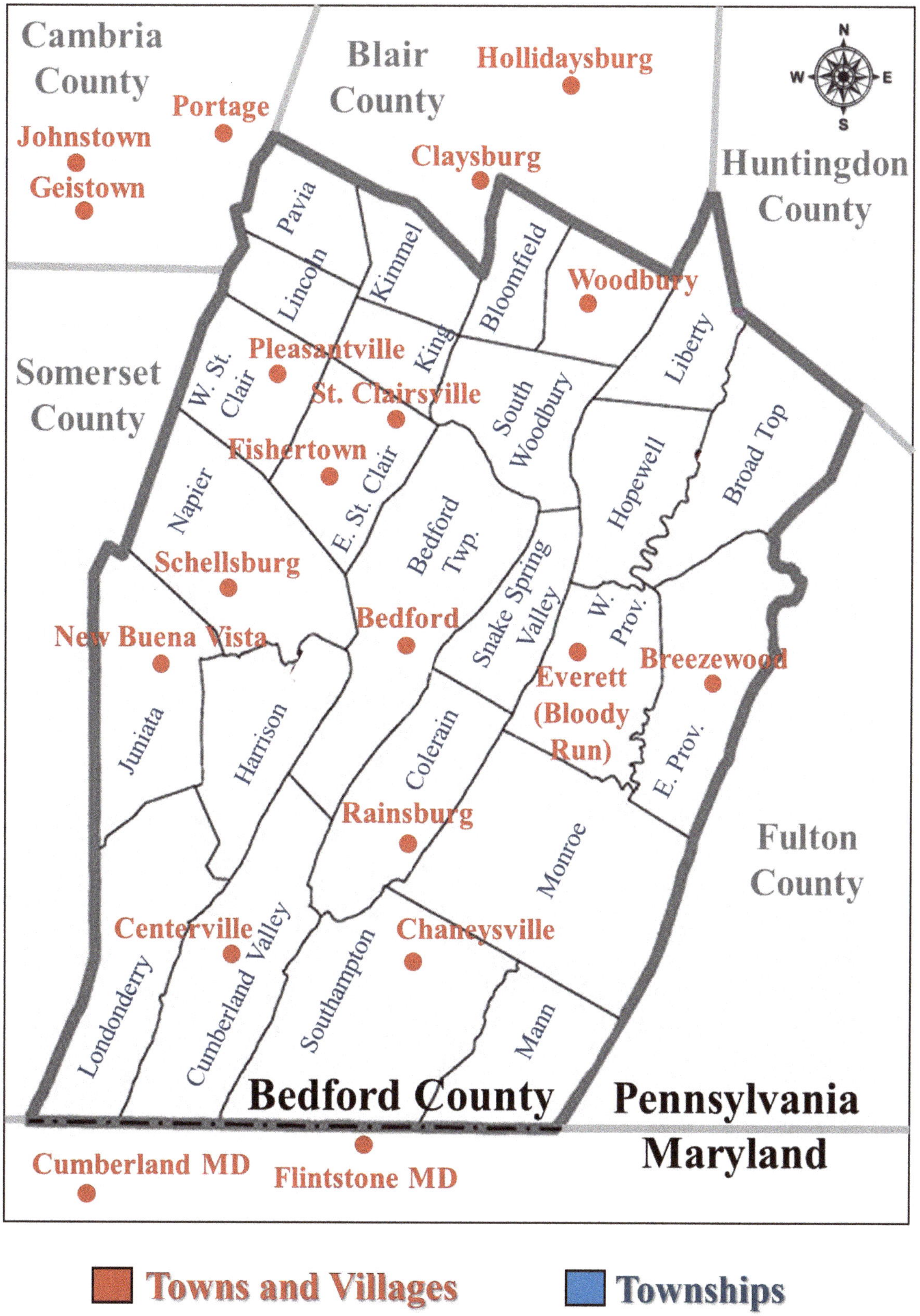

Note: St. Clair Township was divided into East and West St. Clair Townships on September 18, 1875.

If a slave has taken refuge with you, do not hand them over to their master. Let them live among you wherever they like and in whatever town they choose. Do not oppress them.

Deuteronomy 23:15-16.

Chapter 10
Chaneysville
East of Evitts Mountain

Southern parts of Bedford County below Bloody Run (Everett) and the town of Bedford were the most perilous for runaways. Fugitive slave laws required courts to rule on the validity of apprehensions. Slave catchers had a well-earned reputation for being unsavory characters. Most would not hesitate to move a captured runaway quickly back across the Mason Dixon line. Thus, avoiding a Pennsylvania judge who could release the enslaved person and prevent a reward from being collected. Stories circulated of unruly mobs in Pennsylvania attacking slave catchers to free captured enslaved people. For these reasons, slave catchers were especially active near the state line and were familiar with flight paths from Cumberland, Maryland.

One of the known routings from Cumberland ran eastward along the National Road. More folklore than documentation exists in some sections of the Underground Railroad. The areas east of Evitts Mountain are a good example. Some stories offer more questions than answers. None more so than the runaways who perished near Chaneysville.

Most areas east of Evitts Mountain are heavily wooded and rugged. Northward pointing ridges helped guide those willing to traverse difficult terrain. Directions included landmarks such as streams, bridges, structures, rock formations, and gaps between ridges. Caves exist near some paths. One folklore story identified the Saltpetre Cave near Chaneysville as being a shelter for freedom seekers.

Several possible flight paths veer north from Maryland toward the village of Chaneysville. An 1861 map shows some current roads were pathways prior to the Civil War. [1] Nearby streams along many routes provided access to drinking water. Wading through a stream could also throw bloodhounds off a scent if runaways were being tracked. Beans Cove Road runs along the foot of Evitts Mountain before bending toward Chaneysville. Two streams, Rocky Gap Run and Lost Run, flow near Beans Cove road. Two routes cross into Bedford County from the village of Flintstone. Flintstone Creek Road connects to Beans Cove Road about 5 miles north of the state line. Flintstone Creek follows the contour of the road. Route 326 offers the most direct route between Flintstone and Chaneysville. Town Creek flows near route 326.

Flintstone was a well-known stagecoach stop on the National Road. As early as 1835, Jonathan Huddleson kept a tavern for customers of a stagecoach line. Thomas Robinson owned another tavern and a wagon stand. A stagecoach tavern provided better accommodations for the more affluent. A wagon stand was a lower cost option used by most travelers. Both provided food, drink, and lodging. John Piper Jr. was a proprietor of a hotel that became a popular summer resort. After Piper's death in 1871, the Piper Hotel was sold and renamed the Flintstone Hotel. [2]

Rumors exist of the Piper hotel being a station on the Underground Railroad. Today, the hotel is in a badly dilapidated condition. A local person stated a tunnel was once hidden behind a dresser in the hotel's basement. No documentation was found linking John Piper Jr, or the hotel to the Underground Railroad. Records show his son, Watson J. Piper, served as a surgeon in the Union Army during the Civil War. [3] Taverns, inns, and hotels are where slave catchers could receive meals, libations, and overnight accommodations. These locations would not have been ideal Underground Railroad stations.

Folklore exists of chains being fastened to a basement wall of a house just south of the state line between Black Valley Road and Town Creek. The current owner is a descendant of the person who acquired the property for four female enslaved people in 1783. According to the current owner, no chains have existed in the basement during her lifetime. She acknowledged her ancestors were enslavers. Census records do not list enslaved people being on the property from 1820 through 1860. No documentation was found connecting the house to slave catchers. [4]

The Imes property is approximately 4 miles north of the state line on Route 326, also referred to as Chaneysville Road. The family cemetery is a short walk from the road. David Bradley wrote a historical novel, The Chaneysville Incident, in 1981. The book garnered significant notoriety for his narrative of enslaved people believed to be buried in the cemetery. The tragic details of this story remain shrouded in mystery.

The earliest documentation of the story was published in the Bedford Gazette on May 19th, 1964. Bill Jordan wrote an article on historical research conducted by Bedford Township resident Thomas C. Imler. Imler believed the first white settler buried in the county was W. R. Iames in 1758. Imler located a grave marker in a burial ground near Town Creek, around 5 miles south of Chaneysville. Iames was part of a pioneering group of 13 men who came to Bedford County in 1728, decades before Bedford was founded. After covering related historical topics, Bill Jordan mentioned the following.

> Of later date, but perhaps even more interesting, is the legend of the murdered Negroes. The story is that the valley served as one of the stations of the Underground Railroad, which in pre-Civil War times sheltered fleeing Negroes en route from their slave homes in the South to freedom in Canada. On one occasion, Southern pursuers were close on the trail of a band of fleeing slaves in the Valley, and tradition has it that, to save the Negroes from torture and further bondage, and to preserve the Valley itself from reprisal and ruination, eighteen Negroes were slain by the residents. Mr. Imler has found exactly eighteen graves in a set-apart section of the mouldering graveyard. [5]

Harriette Bradley and Thomas C. Imler co-wrote a chapter in the Kernal of Greatness, a bicentennial history book on Bedford County published in 1971. Harriette is the mother of David Bradley. The following is an excerpt from Kernal of Greatness.

> On the Lester Imes farm below Chaneysville, one can still find the markers for twelve or thirteen graves of runaway slaves. Mr. Imes relates that when the slaves realized their pursuers were closing in on them, they begged to be killed rather than go back to the Southland and more servitude. Someone obliged. [6]

Harriet Griffin Dom wrote a brief history of the Imes family in February 1978. Her mother, Nora Imes Griffin, was born on the Imes family property. Harriet listed various spellings of the family name found on documents, including Iiames, Iiams, Iames, Ijams, and Iams. She wrote the following about the story of the runaways.

> There are about 12 stones with names chiseled in. We have identified nine of them. There are about 24 or more graves, many just short ones for children or babies. The story has been passed down by the family that 17 runaway slaves from the south were caught by their owners in that area and they chose to be shot rather than go back. Out by the woods side of the cemetery are many small rocks supposed to be marking their graves. One of the family, now deceased, cleaned up the graveyard and kept it mowed. In 1969 it was almost lost in brush. The Cemetery is kept in fairly good condition by the family who owns the property. [7]

The Pioneer Historical Society organized a series of "Know Your County Tours" in the 1980s. A 1988 Southampton Township tour guide booklet noted the following.

> Twelve escaped slaves (or perhaps more) killed themselves to avoid recapture and were also laid to rest there was long known to every local resident but was fully recorded in writing only when David Bradley's partially speculative novel appeared in 1981. Bradley suggests that "The Chaneysville Incident" occurred shortly before the Civil War. The old mill in which the slaves hid from the bounty hunters lay at the bend of Town Creek just below the cemetery, but only the vague outline of a mill now marks its location. [8]

Jon Baughman wrote a four-part story for the Bedford Gazette and Broad Top Bulletin, nearly 50 years after the Bill Jordan article. Jon and his wife, Judy, met Alton Iames, then 85 years old, and another de-

Chapter 10 - Chaneysville   39

Photograph of the Imes Cemetery. The row of small gravestones to the left and above the tree stump are believed to be the markers for the enslaved people who perished.

Photograph taken near the Imes Cemetery facing Town Creek.

Photograph of Town Creek. The enslaved people may have been traveling along this stream.

Photograph taken near Town Creek facing the Imes Cemetery on the hill.

scendant Ronnie Sparks at the 90-acre farm containing the family cemetery in 2012. Alton was raised on the property by his parents, Lester, and Ora Iames. The following are some of Alton's comments during the tour of the property.

> The story of the escaped slaves goes back many generations in the Iames family and has been told and retold. The exact date the incident took place is not known; however, it was prior to the outbreak of the Civil War (1861). Nor is it known exactly where the slaves were killed, nor who killed them. Some sources say there are 11 or 12 slave graves; Alton suggested there could be as many as 17.

Baughman conducted phone interviews with Alton's sister, Wilda Iames Knisley and cousin, Upton Imes. The following are recollections of Upton from his childhood in the 1940s.

> When we were kids, we played in the vicinity of the cemetery. We were told that escaped slaves were killed close to there and buried there. Nobody knows the year, or the exact details. The story has been retold many times.

I spoke with Upton on August 21st, 2023. Upton confirmed the above information and stated his father, Regia, and uncle Lester retold the story when he was young. Upton mentioned he has recollections of his grandfather, Upton Imes (same name), as a small boy. The elder Upton's father was Aaron, who likely resided on the Imes family property or lived nearby at the time of the tragedy.

The following are excerpts of comments Wilda made during the interview.

> My understanding is that the fugitive slaves got that far (the Iames farm), chased by bounty hunters, and they did not want to go back. They asked the Iames family to do away with them and they asked to be buried there (on the farm). They must have followed Town Creek north. The old home place is across the creek from the Iames cemetery.

> Wilda pointed out the Iames family has always been kind to strangers. They would take anybody in and feed them. The main highway went past our house. Hobos, tramps, and others often passed by, and they would stop and ask for something to eat. My mother always fed them. I remember a man stopping about supper time and asked if he could sleep in the barn. Mom fixed a plate of food for him and even offered breakfast, but early the next morning, he moved on.

Jon Baughman provided the following commentary in his article on who may have assisted in the request from the runaways to end their lives.

> In my research I have rumors of a name or two, but that would be speculation, and it did not involve members of the Iames family. But it was members of the Iames family who took the time to try to match husbands with wives, children with mothers, and so on, and bury them in that manner, rather than at random.

Baughman researched Southampton Township census records for the article. The 1830 census listed two black females in the township. In 1840, the census recorded two black males under the age of 10 and one black male between the age of 20 and 30. All three lived with different white families. A mulatto family was also listed in 1840. The Amos Harris household included two adults and six children. The 1850 census records show Amos Harris and two family members had moved to Bedford Township. [9] Only one black female was listed on the 1850 Southampton Township census. The 1860 census listed two blacks living in the township.

The following is some historical information on the Iames family and their property. James Spurgeon received a patent for the Iames property on September 29, 1764. This tract of land, named "Spurgeon's Choice" was initially part of Frederick County, MD. The Mason-Dixon survey in 1767 placed the property in Bedford County, PA. A grist mill was built on the property along Town Creek by James Spurgeon prior to selling the property to William Iames I in 1783. The grist mill was destroyed in a flood after the Civil War.

The 1790 Bedford County census listed four enslaved people on the William Iames property. The 1796 Colerain Township tax records for William Jams cited three enslaved people. In this early era, Southampton was part of Colerain Township. Jams may have been another spelling of the last name. Iames also owned property in Maryland. A William Ijames was listed in the 1800 Washington County Census as the enslaver of one person. Washington County encompasses Hagerstown and Hancock. The 1810 Allegany Census listed a William Iams, who was an enslaver of 3 people. Many spellings of the last name call into question if all this cited information can be attributed to the same individual. William Iames I passed away in Allegany County, Maryland in 1831. He was survived by three sons, Amos, William II, and Jesse.

William Iames II, was born in 1785 and married Ruth Perrin in 1808. William II was listed as residing on the property in the 1810 Southampton Township Census. There are no records of William II ever owning enslaved people. He inherited the Southampton Township property when his father died in 1831. William II passed in 1858. His wife preceded him in death in 1853. A son Aaron was born in 1819. The 1860 census records and an 1861 Bedford County map show Aaron Imes living on the family property at that time. [10]

Much of what we know about the story of the runaways was provided by Lester Iames and his brother, Regia. Lester and Regia's grandfather, Aaron, likely lived nearby or resided on the family property during the time of the story. It appears Aaron may have helped bury the runaways. Choosing the family cemetery instead of another part of the property possibly indicates sympathy for the freedom seekers.

Working from the assumption, the basic parameters of the story are accurate, many questions remain. When did the tragedy take place? How unusual was it for a large group of enslaved people to flee together? What triggered this desperate escape attempt? Why would a family request to end their lives rather than return to bondage? Was this family receiving aid from the Underground Railroad, or fleeing without the help of others?

In the early decades of the 1800s, single males made most escape attempts. Over time, word spread of

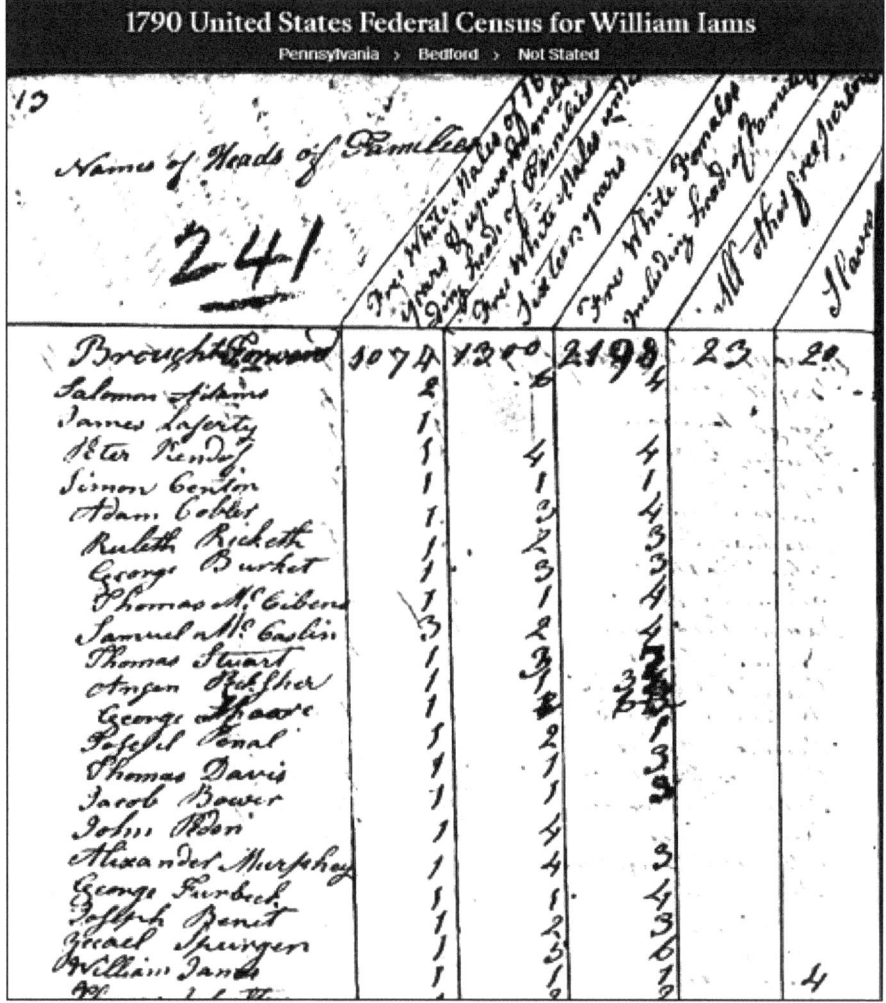

The 1790 Bedford County Census for William Iams listed 4 slaves on the bottom right of the image. (Ancestry.com)

successful escapes and enslaved people seeking freedom became more aware of people willing to help. By the 1840s, families fleeing slavery together became more common. The 1850s are believed to have been the most active period for people fleeing slavery. [11]

A North-Side view of Slavery, published in 1856, compiled stories of enslaved people who escaped to Canada. This book provides insights on what triggered some escape attempts. The following are excerpts of a life story told by George Johnson.

> I was raised near Harper's Ferry. We went to work at sunrise and quit work between sundown and dark. Some were sold from my master's farm, and many from the neighborhood. If a man did anything out of the way, he was in more danger of being sold than of being whipped. The slaves were always afraid of being sold South. The Southern masters were believed to be much worse than those about us. [12]

Work in the baking heat of cotton fields in the deep south was widely believed to be a more brutal existence by enslaved people in other regions. Two events led to cotton becoming a dominate cash crop which increased the demand for enslaved people. Eli Whitney invented the cotton gin in 1794. His invention revolutionized cotton production by speeding up the process of removing seeds from fiber. The Creek Indian War of 1813-1814 opened up vast areas of Georgia, Alabama, Mississippi, and Tennessee to white settlement and the establishment of cotton plantations. [13]

An overwhelming fear among enslaved people was being sold. Thoughts of husbands being permanently separated from wives and parents from children were terrifying. Estates were occasionally liquidated after the death of an enslaver to divide assets among descendants. Sheriff sales also liquidated estates to settle debts. Fear of heartbreaking family separations had the potential to trigger a tragic situation.

The Underground Railroad was a loosely formed network of people who helped enslaved people when aid was requested. We will never know if these runaways reached the Imes property by chance, as slave catchers were closing in or if they were aware, the Imes family would provide food and shelter. From a geographical perspective, it seems likely at least one Underground Railroad station would have existed near the village of Chaneysville.

Photograph of the Grist mill on the Imes property along Town Creek. Lester Imes is pictured 3rd from the left laying on the spoke. (Eric Wise)

*Drawing of the escape of Patrick and Abraham.
(Sandy Vale Memorial Gardens)*

Chapter 11

Bloody Run and Rainsburg
A story of the Barndollar Family

Two cited Underground Railroad routings extend from Chaneysville. The village of Rainsburg is 6 miles north on route 326. Everett can be reached in 15 miles via Black Valley Road. The name of the town has changed five times. In 1738, Everett was referred to as Aliquippa, an Indian name. The area is believed to have been the site of an Indian village of considerable significance. In 1758, trail blazers completed the 200-mile historic Forbes Road connecting Carlisle and Pittsburgh. According to folklore, an Indian massacre took place along a creek that runs through the middle of Everett while the road was being cut. After the massacre, the area became known as Bloody Run. Around 1770, widow Betsy Tussey opened a tavern, and the village was referred to as Tusseys. In 1795, founder Michael Barndollar named the town Waynesburg, after Revolutionary War hero Anthony Wayne. But the name never stuck with residents, and in 1860, the town was renamed Bloody Run. The name changed again to Everett in 1873. [1]

One of the most detailed pursuit stories of enslaved people in Bedford County began in Bloody Run. In early February 1837, two brothers, Patrick and Abraham, escaped from the Fruit Hill farm of Colonel John Sherrard in Virginia. They were pursued across the Pennsylvania state line by slave catchers, John Compston and Edward Maxwell. The following is a verbatim excerpt from the diary of James Blackburn, dated May 14th, 1837.

> About the beginning of the year 1837 two runaway slaves from Virginia, aged respectively twenty and twenty-one years, being brothers, and the property of one master, accompanied by two others whose residence was unknown, arrived at Bloody Run and took lodging for the night at a private house. Their pursuers came upon them during the night and threatened violence upon them if they did not surrender. The negroes resolved to fight for their liberty, and gave terrific battle, which was of short duration. The last named two, making least resistance, were taken, and not heard of afterward. The former made their escape, after one receiving a pistol shot wound on his cheek. They made their way to Bucks Town (St. Clairsville), where they stopped at the house of a man of their own color; but they were pursued by a recruited force and were there, in a manner, taken, but they again resisted, and after another pitched battle escaped without much injury to themselves, but having wounded one of their pursuers in the hand with a hatchet—this man, J. G., being a citizen of the place, and having taken active part in the effort of capturing.

> They then took what is called the Johnstown Road, still pursued by eight or ten men, but were not overtaken until they reached one Heltzel's, in the mountain, a distance of eighteen or twenty miles from the scene of their last engagement. Here they remained for a night, or part of a night, but on arising in the morning, and before they were dressed, they saw their pursuers approaching the house. They hurried into their clothes and met them at the door, where another encounter was had, in which the man of the house assisted the pursuers, one of whom, of brutal nature, seized a small ax and struck one black several blows, one of which was on the head, which at length brought him to the ground, when some of them were about to lay hold upon him and bind him; his brother, seeing this, rushed in and pulled them away from him, and by violent exertions kept them from their purpose until the brother arose, and they together again succeeded in making their escape, but were followed with increased

vigilance for some distance, when they were met by two young men who had been hunting and had guns with them. These hunters were pressed into service by the would-be captors, with orders that if the negroes could not be taken otherwise to shoot them, which they did, wounding one of them in the shoulder, the ball lodging in his chest, and the other receiving a wound in his knee, severely injuring him. This cruel treatment retarded their progress, and their pursuers again advanced upon them and no doubt thought the prize was won, for, one of the blacks having fallen to the ground from the effects of his wounds, the aforementioned J. G. (the man who had gotten hurt in the hand) was about to spring upon him, and called for one of his accomplices to cut his (G.'s) bridle rein with which to tie the captive. The other black suggested not to cut the bridle, 'for,' says he, 'you don't have us yet,' and, accompanying his suggestion with the throwing of a stone, Mr. G. received the missile on his breast and dropped to the ground. The prostrate slave, seeing this ray of hope for his escape, arose, and, while the pursuers' attention was turned to G., their comrade, the fugitives moved forward as rapidly as they could go. They next arrived at the home of William Sleek, who was much alarmed to see their condition, and earnestly inquired what was the matter, or whether they had murdered someone. They replied that they had not, nor did not mean to kill anyone; and they briefly told him their tragic story. He said that if that was the case, they might come in, and he would protect them from further assaults; but in a few minutes, their pursuers arrived, and Mr. G. was so infuriated that he went on like a madman. He told Sleek that he was a sworn officer and had authority to take the negroes (he being a constable), and threatened what he would do if they were not given up. Sleek coolly told him that he disregarded his authority, for he had no legal process to take them, his warrant not being renewed in this state; and that if they proceeded further, they must go legally about it.

In the meantime, Sleek sent word to Johnstown, from which a number of blacks issued and came to Sleek's, which alarmed some of the pursuers, and especially the overseers, who suspected a massacre, but Sleek calmed their apprehension and told them they would not be injured, nor were they. They withdrew, however, from further pursuit.

The blacks had their wounds dressed, and were soon conveyed on a sled to Johnstown, where some individuals espousing their cause took them in charge, and issued out warrants for their assailants, whereupon some fled the country, others gave bail, etc. Two hundred dollars reward was offered for G. The master of the slaves offered three hundred dollars reward for their capture, and a few hard-hearted wretches made further effort to reclaim them, when it became necessary to remove them to greater safety, and they were transferred to the Quaker settlement in St. Clair township and from there they were conveyed to Center County, thence to Clearfield county, and finally on toward Canada, where they probably arrived without further molestation, and remained free from the accursed state of human bondage. [2]

In the diary entry, James Blackburn noted the two brothers, Patrick and Abraham, and two other enslaved people were provided shelter at a private house in Bloody Run. No information has been found on the location of the house or the identity of the owner.

A second pitched battle took place in Bucks Town (St. Clairsville) at the house of a black resident. The 1840 Census recorded only one black man in St. Clair Township, Samuel Luskey. He was listed as being between 36 and 55 years old. The residence included an adult female and two children under 10 years old. No other information was found on Samuel or his family.

The diary entry referred to an enraged slave catcher from St. Clairsville as J. G. There were 3 men with the initials J. G. on the 1840 St. Clair Township census. One man was listed as being between the age of 90 and 100. This individual can be excluded for obvious reasons. A second man was listed between the age of 30 and 40 with a wife and two small children at home. This couple married in 1836, the year before the Patrick and Abraham incident. The wife was the daughter of Quaker parents. Her husband later volunteered in the Civil War at age 50. He was over the age limit for new recruits, so he apparently misrepresented his age to join. Circumstantial factors make it less likely this man was the slave catcher referenced in the story. A third man with the initials J. G. was listed between the age of 20 and 30 with a wife and small child in the home. This man died accidentally when he fell off a wagon at age 56. It appears this man may have been the slave catcher, but definitive proof cannot be established. A possibility remains of another man with the initials J. G. moving out of the township prior to the 1840 census. [3]

Patrick and Abraham were pursued from St. Clairsville to Cambria County by eight or ten men. Patrick and Abraham stayed part of the night at the home of a Helzel in Richland Township. A Johnstown Tribune-Democrat article identified this person as George Helsel. [4] Two different George Helsel's are listed on the 1840 Richland Township census.

William Sleek provided considerable help to Patrick and Abraham at his home in Geistown, near Johnstown. William is possibly the most well-known Underground Railroad agent in Cambria County. After reaching Johnstown, Patrick and Abraham traveled back to St. Clair Township to a safer location within the Quaker community. Moving freedom seekers in a zigzag manner, even retracing routes, was a common tactic used to throw off slave catchers.

Judge William M. Hall provided details of a tragic story between slave catchers and two enslaved men a few miles south of Bloody Run. No date was provided on the confrontation. The following is a verbatim excerpt of the story published in 1890.

> In Monroe or West Providence township, a few miles south of Bloody Run (now Everett), two fugitive slaves were overtaken by a Maryland or Virginia slave-hunter, aided by some Bedford County assistants, men who were on the *qui vive* for a reward, and who followed the business of slave-catching for gain. One of the slaves was armed with an old single-barreled pistol, which, as the captors approached, he drew and exhibited as he retreated; the captors were armed with pistols and a rifle, which latter implement was brought into use and one of the slaves was shot at long range. He died and was buried near where he fell, and the survivor was taken south. There was no coroner's inquest, nor published notice of this occurrence in any way, and very little comment upon it in the neighborhood. [5]

The location of this story was presumably on or near Black Valley Road. Local historians reference different folklore stories on the origins of the name Black Valley and Black Valley Road. One narrative states the name came from a black family who hid out in the valley in the 1700s. Another story cites the name originated from a black family who drowned near where they were camping. There is a legend of a lost black community in Black Valley. Lore exists of Native Americans citing virgin tree cover so dense, no light could shine on the valley floor. Another narrative is the valley was named after the Black Forest in Germany by early settlers. Most of the folklore associates the name of the valley with black people.

Many runaways who crossed the state line east of Evitts Mountain passed through Rainsburg and Bloody Run. Roads from both led to known safe houses in Bedford, Snake Spring Valley, and Woodbury. Harriette Bradley referenced a station near the Narrows Bridge just south of route 30, about 9 miles from Rainsburg. Harriette noted, "The trek up the eastern side (of Evitts Mountain) brought the fugitives through Chaneysville, Rainsburg, and along the present route 326. Sometimes they were kept in a stone house near the former Jansens Farm supply store. They were brought to Bedford when the time was right." [6] A 14-mile route also existed between Rainsburg and Bloody Run. Little was ever written about the people in Rainsburg and Bloody Run who helped enslaved people. The following information appeared in a 2010 Juneteenth program pamphlet.

> In 1787, Michael Barndollar moved to the area we now know as Everett. He received the formal charter for the town in 1795. Michael established many of the longstanding businesses of the town. In 1801, he built the Union Hotel on Main Street.
>
> It's known that Michael Barndollar kept female African American slaves as house servants. Supposedly, these slaves were "well" treated. Eventually, the entire Barndollar family changed their attitudes toward slavery. It's even known that Nelle Fry, an ex-Barndollar slave, lived as a free woman with the family from 1860 to 1870.
>
> Eventually Michael Barndollar's son, Peter, established an Underground Railroad station at the Tannery Weigh Station - today known as Dunkle's Barber Shop. The Zimmerman Hardware building was the actual tannery processing plant. Peter Barndollar's son, Jacob,

also became an active conductor on the Underground Railroad. Jacob was a very important family leader. We suspect Jacob encouraged other Bedford County family members, such as Catherine Barndollar in Rainsburg, to establish safe houses in their communities. Today multiple generations of Barndollar family tell stories of runaway slaves who were kept in the attic of their weigh station. [7]

Michael Barndollar was born in Germantown, near Philadelphia in 1740 and died in 1818. In 1796, per terms of the 1780 Pennsylvania Gradual Abolition Act, Michael Barndollar registered an enslaved woman named Sall, and a daughter named Philis. In 1804, Sall's second child, Dina, was registered. The 1810 census listed no blacks living in the Barndollar household. It is not known if Sall and her children were still enslaved by 1810. [8] Michael Barndollar's son, Peter, was born in Philadelphia in 1778 and passed in 1858. No blacks were listed as living in the Peter Barndollar household on the census records from 1820 to 1840. Peter's son, Jacob T. was born in Bloody Run in 1809 and lived until 1883. The Barndollar clan owned significant amounts of real estate and several businesses in Bloody Run. Two Barndollar family members also served as postmasters in the town prior to the Civil War. [9]

Registration of Sall and a child named Philis in 1798 by Michael Barndollar. (Pennsylvania Historical and Museum Commission)

The 2010 Juneteenth pamphlet information on the Barndollar involvement in the Underground Railroad can be traced to two granddaughters of Jacob T. Barndollar: Eliza Ellis Barndollar (1883-1973) and Sarah Barndollar Lloyd (1881-1966). The sisters lived together in their family home on Main Street in Everett after Sarah's husband had passed away in 1949. Eliza never married. Their great niece, Laurie Ann Yingling (1943-2009), often stayed with the sisters during summer months while growing up in Alexandria, VA. Laurie passed along stories retold to her by Eliza and Sarah at Barndollar family reunions. [10]

Samuel Williams, Catherine Barndollar's husband, owned farmland surrounding Rainsburg and founded the Rainsburg Seminary. The 1860 census and an 1861 map showed the family owned a boarding house near the seminary. Catherine's brother, William Barndollar, owned a store in Rainsburg in the 1840s and 1850s. [11] During the Underground Railroad era, many runaways were transported in wagons hauling agricultural products, store merchandise, and leather for tannery processing. No stories survive connecting the extended Barndollar family to these activities.

Nelle Fry is listed on the 1850 Census as an 11-year-old free mulatto girl born in Pennsylvania. She was living in the multi-generational Barndollar family home of Peter and Ann Barndollar, son James M. his wife Eliza, and their children. James was the proprietor of a store in Bloody Run. Around the time Nelle was born, only seven free blacks were listed in the 1840 West Providence-Bloody Run census. None had the last name Fry. The 1860 Census showed Nelle Fry living with the James M. Barndollar family. The 1870 census listed both Nelle and a 14-year-old white girl from Ohio, Martha Hedges, being domestic servants in the James M. Barndollar household.

In the 1880 Everett census, Nelle shared a residence with a 34-year-old white female, Charlotte Whitfield. This census report stated Nelle's parents were born in Virginia. This clue opens several possibilities of how Nelle came to live with the Barndollar family. [12] By 1840, there were only 64 blacks listed as being en-

Chapter 11 - Bloody Run and Rainsburg   49

James M. Barndollar, (History of Bedford, Somerset and Fulton Counties)

Undated photo of the Jacob T. Barndollar house built in 1858. The Barndollar tannery weigh station is shown behind the residence on Main Street in Everett. (Barbara Sponsler Miller)

Undated photograph of Rainsburg. (Patricia Morgart)

Samuel Williams boarding house on Route 326 in Rainsburg.

Catherine Barndollar Williams. (Barbara Sponsler Miller)

slaved on the Pennsylvania census. A 1788 amendment to the Pennsylvania Gradual Abolition Act of 1780, declared enslaved people owned by people who intended to move or settle in Pennsylvania permanently, should be declared immediately free.[13] No other records on Nelle Fry were found.

Further research determined the Zimmerman Hardware building would not have been the Barndollar tannery processing plant. This Zimmerman building was constructed after the Underground Railroad era. The Barndollar tannery building, or buildings, would have stood very near to the tannery weigh station, which is still standing.

The involvement of the extended Barndollar family in supporting enslaved people appears to make sense. It is unlikely the most prominent families in Bloody Run and Rainsburg were unaware of and did not approve of supporting runaways passing through their small communities. The connections between family members in Rainsburg and Bloody Run appear unusually close. Samuel D. Williams and Jacob T. Barndollar, married the sister of the other man. Jacob married Eliza Williams in 1834, the same year Samuel married Catherine Barndollar. Both couples had three sons who volunteered in the Union Army. After the Civil War, Samuel and Catherine's eldest son, Jacob Barndollar Williams, became one of the most well-known business owners in Everett's history.[14]

Ten sons of the Barndollar-Williams clan fought in the Civil War. The following are details of the enlistments.

No.	Name	Age	Rank	Regiment	Casualty	Casualty Battle
1	Barndollar, Jacob W	21	Pvt.	PA 133rd Inf.	Wounded	Fredericksburg
			Pvt.	PA 186th Inf.		
2	Barndollar, James E	18	Pvt.	PA 133rd Inf.	KIA	Fredericksburg
3	Barndollar, James J	23	1st Sgt.	PA 133rd Inf.		
4	Barndollar, John W	23	Corp.	PA 13th Inf.		
			Pvt.	PA 5th H. Art.		
5	Barndollar, Martin D	18	Pvt.	PA 133rd Inf.		
			Corp.	PA 194th Inf.		
			Sgt.	PA 83rd Inf.		
6	Barndollar, William G	18	Pvt.	PA 194th Inf.		
7	Barndollar, William P	21	2nd Lt.	PA 13th Inf.		
			1st Lt.	PA 76th Inf.	POW	
8	Williams, Jacob B	26		PA 133rd Inf.		
9	Williams, John H	24	Sgt.	PA 8th Res.		
			1st Lt.	PA 194th Inf.		
10	Williams, Samuel D	22	2nd Lt.	PA 133rd Inf.		
			2nd Lt.	PA 194th Inf.		

There were many terrible days for the Union Army during the war, perhaps none worse than December 13th, 1862. On that day, wave after wave of Union soldiers were cut down during charges on the impregnable rebel defenses at Marye's Heights during the battle of Fredericksburg. Six Barndollar and Williams sons enlisted in the 133rd Pennsylvania Infantry and took part in the near suicidal charges. It was a tragic day for many local families. Sixty-five Bedford County soldiers were casualties at Fredericksburg.[15]

Recollections of Bygone Days in the Cove are a multivolume series of booklets containing articles written by Ella M. Snowberger for the Morrisons Cove Herald. Ella's articles were based on personal interviews with older citizens in local communities. The following are excerpts from an interview with Sally Barndollar Fockler, younger sister of Jacob W. and James E. Barndollar.

> Many boys enlisted. That was a thrilling time, fraught with anguish, when the boys donned their blue uniforms and went to the war. It was certainly one of the most significant days in the history of Everett. The company of young recruits assembled on the public square. Flags waved, speeches were made, mothers wept, and the band blared martial music. The oath of

loyalty was taken.

At length, the command to march rang out. The band broke into the strains of "Tramp, Tramp, the Boys are Marching." Stepping to the music, the boys, a fine sight in the new blue uniforms and glittering brass buttons, marched down the street to the Barndollar railway station. Yes, it was the Barndollar station then because the Barndollars founded Bloody Run, now Everett.

There the soldiers crowded into the coaches of the train. "Goodbye, my boy, goodbye!" called out parents, brothers, sisters, sweethearts, and neighbors. O, what a heart-breaking chorus that was. Grave young faces clustered from the windows and the flutter of white handkerchiefs signaled farewell as long as the train remained in sight.

John Barndollar and his wife and family awaited news from the front. To this day, Sally Barndollar Fockler declared the suspense and sorrow incident to the Civil war shorted her mother's life. She died at 53. Father haunted the post office in the evenings, both hopeful and fearful of the news that might be awaiting him. The Ott brothers at the post office promised to let him know at once if any letters came.

On December 22, 1862, Mike Ott came to the Barndollar home with a letter. "Read it," requested Mr. Barndollar. Breaking the seal, Mr. Ott read the official notification: "John and Mary Barndollar. Your son James killed in action and your son Jacob wounded and in the hospital."

Father at once went to the hospital in Virginia. From the lips of Jacob, he learned James had been killed in the holocaust at Fredericksburg. Under fire, Jacob said, James always stood with his gun pointed, his body poised forward with a look of eagerness as if thinking: "Come on you rebels, I'll get you." He stood like that on the field of Fredericksburg alongside Jacob. A bullet pierced him. He fell to the ground, his lips quivering with the tremor of death. Before Jacob could lift him up or reach him, a bullet struck him in the breast, and he too fell unconscious.

No trace of James' body was ever found. Members of the family have never ceased to search for a clue to his resting place. Even Sally Barndollar Fockler's children and grandchildren are still trying to uncover some information that might lead them to locate his grave. Jacob believed that James' body found final disposition in a trench. In retreat, under fire, he had seen the dead collected and rolled into a hastily dug trench and covered over without ceremony or markers left to indicate the place. Jacob was in the hospital nine weeks. Following his recovery, he returned to the army and served for the duration of the war. Another brother, William G., was also in the war. [16]

Photograph of Jacob W. Barndollar taken shortly after suffering a wound at the battle of Fredericksburg. (Ronn Palm)

Black residents along Underground Railroad routes often helped freedom seekers. No stories survive of black families in Colerain Township (Rainsburg) or West Providence Township (Bloody Run) aiding runaways. Twelve blacks were listed in the 1850 Colerain Township census, including members of the Ray, Louden, and Brown families. Eleven blacks were listed on the 1860 census, including the extended Boaston family. John, Samuel, and James Boaston lived on separate farm properties.

Eighteen blacks lived in West Providence Township

(Bloody Run) in 1850, including members of the McNeil, Vesay, and Wonder families. Two blacks were listed on the 1860 census, including Nelle Fry.

The Barndollar family conversion from enslavers to Underground Railroad supporters is a curious subject. Differences in values sometimes vary from generation to generation. What triggered the change in the Barndollar family is unknown. The Barndollars were founders of the Methodist Church in Bloody Run. Michael Barndollar provided funding for the first church building between 1810 and 1812 on the corner of East First and Hopewell streets. [17] It is possible Methodist doctrine influenced the way slavery was viewed by the family.

John Wesley, cofounder of Methodism, condemned slavery in a pamphlet titled "Thoughts upon Slavery" in 1784. This influential document condemned slavery and warned those involved would one day face the wrath of God's judgement. [18] Five years later, the church issued a memorandum of sins to be avoided. The list included: "the buying or selling of the bodies or souls of men, women, or children, with an intention to enslave them." In 1816, the General Conference adopted a resolution: "no slaveholder shall be eligible to any official station in our Church hereafter, where the laws of the state in which he lives will admit emancipation and permit the liberated slave to enjoy freedom." [19]

No further details were uncovered on Barndollar involvement in the Underground Railroad. Only brief word-of-mouth mentions survived through the generations. It's not known why the Barndollar's never wrote about their efforts to help enslaved people. The Barndollar's, along with many families in Bedford County, were deeply affected when issues surrounding slavery plunged the country into a terrible Civil War. One member of the Barndollar family never returned home. Others likely returned home scarred from witnessing horrors. One of the Barndollar soldiers, Martin D. Barndollar, deeded the Mt. Pisgah A.M.E. church in Everett to the congregation for $1.00 in 1888. [20] Perhaps a desire to move on from all issues relating to the war were among the reasons they chose not to write about Underground Railroad activities.

Martin Barndollar family photograph circa 1920. Top row: Mary, Sarah, Martin Jr., Clara and Eliza. Bottom row: Martin Sr., Betty and Elizabeth. Martin Sr. is the son of Jacob T. Barndollar. The daughters of Martin Sr., Sarah and Eliza, retold the story of the Barndollar involvement in the Underground Railroad. (Barbara Sponsler Miller)

Chapter 11 - Bloody Run and Rainsburg 53

Undated Bedford Gazette photograph of the Barndollar tannery weigh station. This building also served as a kitchen for Union Soldiers who retreated to Bloody Run after being routed in Winchester, Virginia during the Gettysburg campaign in 1863. (Barbara Sponsler Miller)

Current photograph of the Barndollar tannery weigh station and the Jacob T. Barndollar house.

54   *The Underground Railroad in Bedford County Pennsylvania*

(left) John C. Morgart house. (Morgart family tree - Ancestry.com). (right) The Morgart house stood near this mailbox along Route 220.

Elizabeth Beegle Morgart and John C. Morgart. (Ancestry.com)

(left) Morgart Inn and Tavern built in 1791. (Morgart family tree on Ancestry.com). (right) The tavern once stood north of the Providence Lutheran Church on Route 220.

Chapter 12
Cumberland Valley

Once enslaved runaways reached Cumberland, Maryland, the Mason-Dixon line was only six miles away. Many freedom seekers chose the shortest distance to the Pennsylvania state line and crossed into Cumberland Valley Township. Slave catchers were also well aware of this direct routing. Cumberland Valley is framed by Wills Mountain on the west and Evitts Mountain on the east. From the state line, the town of Bedford is less than 25 miles away. A host of free blacks and John Cessna Morgart, a white tavern owner, provided help to many of the enslaved people who took this route into Bedford County.

Harriette Bradley identified John Cessna Morgart as part of the Underground Railroad in a Bedford County Press article in 1976. The following is an excerpt from a paper written by Harriette Bradley on local black history.

> John Morgart lived in the area on Route 220 where the sign points to the Cumberland Dam. Mr. Morgart was an agent and his home still inhabited was also an underground station. [1]

The home of John C. Morgart was located less than 3 miles from the state line on the west side of Route 220. Morgart owned a tavern originally built by Henry Williams in 1791. The Morgart Tavern stood on the east side of Route 220, north of the Providence Lutheran Church, around 8 miles from the family residence. John Morgart married Elizabeth Beegle in 1837. Both were raised in Colerain Township. [2] It is unknown when John and Elizabeth Morgart moved to Cumberland Valley. The family is listed on the 1850 Cumberland Valley census. A story exists of enslaved people being captured at a tavern in Cumberland Valley, possibly the one owned by the Morgart family. The following is the excerpt from a book written by Judge William M. Hall in 1890.

> I relate one instance upon the authority of Dr. William H. Watson II. I do not recall the exact date, but it must have been in 1851, or '52, or '53. An entire family, consisting of a mother and several children (it runs in my mind that there were seven in all), who belonged in Virginia, not far from Cumberland, Maryland, escaped. They were to be sold; the necessity of the settlement of an estate required this. The mother, dreading a separation, fled northward with her little ones, and with a horse which she took along to enable them to travel. They were captured six or eight miles south of Bedford on a cold day in December. The doctor saw them in the hands of their captors at Centreville, halfway between Bedford and Cumberland. They stopped there at the tavern to warm. Among the children was a lad of sixteen or seventeen years, who had on his stockingless feet an old pair of tight boots that looked like a cast-off pair of gentleman's boots. To secure him, his captors had bound his feet under the horse's body. His feet were frozen, and when his boots were pulled off, the skin and soles of his feet came with them. No man dared to question the captors or interfere with them in any way. [3]

John Morgart dealt with family tragedy during the Civil War. In March 1864, John, his wife Elizabeth and seven children moved to Illinois. Two weeks after arriving in Illinois, Elizabeth died. An older son, William Morgart, enlisted in the 18th Pennsylvania Cavalry in 1862. He died in a POW camp in Florence, South Carolina, in November 1864. John Morgart passed in 1897 and is buried in Shawnee Mound, Missouri. [4]

Many black citizens in Bedford County lived in Cumberland Valley Township, Bedford Township and Bedford Borough. The following are the 1840, 1850, and 1860 census records.

	1840	1850	1860
Cumberland Valley Township	54	68	86
Bedford Township	114	118	177
Bedford Borough	54	68	52
Other Bedford Co. Townships and Boroughs	141	151	179

A professor of history at Ohio State University, Wilbur H. Siebert, wrote a seminal book on the Underground Railroad. "The Underground Railroad from Slavery to Freedom" was published in 1898. While researching the book, Siebert reached out to many people, requesting their recollections. The following is a verbatim transcript of an extraordinary letter Siebert received from Bedford County. The letter was dictated by Wyatt Perry to John W. Rouse, who typed the letter on December 23, 1895.

> You will find inclosed a statement of Wyatt Perry, as to the Underground Railroad station between Cumberland, Md., and Bedford, Pa.
>
> I lived close to the Mason-Dixon line in Bedford County, Pa., on a farm called the Bear Tract Station. The fugitives would come there from Cumberland, (Md.). I lived about five miles from Cumberland, (Md.). About twelve years before the war, Jacob Dicken, who belonged to a man by the name of Willeby, who had sold Dicken, and had the money for him. Willeby told Dicken to put his team away, and take a basket and a note to Mr. Hammond, of Cumberland, (Md.). Dicken was to be handed over to a Georgia man and taken south. Dicken found out he was sold. He took the basket and note and threw it in the creek, went home, kissed his wife, bid her goodby, told her he was sold, and would have to leave. The following Sunday morning, he came up to our place, the Bear Tract, for us to get him away. So we took Jacob down to Mr. Heddington, a schoolteacher, and got him to draw the necessary freedom papers, from mine and Mr. Gross's. Mr. Gross took him up on the mountain, and put him on the right road. The following Monday, his master started after him and followed him to Canada, but Dicken happened to get on the boat before his master. The master came back home and died in a short time.
>
> There was a man came to our house from Virginia. Rev. Nelson Davis brought him to Bedford, Pa. I brought two from Bear Tract to Bedford, PA., and gave them over to Harry Marshall, and they were passed on over the underground railroad; also a man and his wife. I sent a boy from Frostburg, Md., over the underground railroad to Rev. John Fidler of Bedford, Pa. The hottest time we had was in getting the man that belonged to James Parsons of Virginia away. It was a habeas corpus case, tried in the county of Blair, state of Pennsylvania, under the Fugitive Slave Law. The fugitive was defended by David Hoffous, Esq. The Mitchel family consisted of nine. I brought them from this side of Cumberland, to Henry Barks, of Bedford. On account of this family, I was threatened and had to leave Bedford, and in doing so, lost my horses and all I had. I went into Blair County, Pennsylvania. I have more I can send to you if you so desire. [5]

Wyatt Perry was born in Allegheny County (Cumberland), Maryland, around 1819. His wife, Martha Norris, was born in Frederick County, Maryland in 1830. It is not known if Wyatt and Martha were born into slavery. Wyatt stated he lived on the Bear Tract Station Farm near the Mason-Dixon line around 12 years before the Civil War. Many black residents of this community were once enslaved people on the Thomas O.B. Carter plantation in Virginia. The 1850 Cumberland Valley Census listed an enclave of 64 black people living in 10 separate neighboring dwellings. The 1860 census reported Wyatt was a blacksmith and a property owner in Bedford Township. Wyatt volunteered in the 3rd Regiment of the U.S.C.T. in July 1863, and mustered out in October 1865, after the Civil War ended. Wyatt passed away in 1899 and is buried in the Mt. Ross Cemetery in Bedford. [6]

John W. Rouse, who typed the recollections of Wyatt Perry, was a black attorney in Bedford. Rouse maintained a law office on West Pitt Street and was the son of a well-known abolitionist and Underground Railroad agent, Eli Rouse.

Little information was found on the individuals cited in the first story of the letter. A search on the name Jacob Dicken, who fled to Canada, yielded no results. Only one man with a similar name to Willeby was found as living in Allegany County (Cumberland) during this era. A James Willoughby is listed on the 1840 Allegany Census. No enslaved people were recorded on the census report for this man. There were no records found for a person named Heddington. A somewhat similar name was recorded in the 1850 Cumberland Valley Census. John Hendrickson was listed as a farmer, born in Maryland in 1823. It was common for teachers to live on farms in this era, but it can't be determined if John Hendrickson is the person who forged the slave pass. The name Gross was not found on census records. Jacob Dicken, being taken up on the mountain and put on the right road, is an interesting detail about the Underground Railroad in Cumberland Valley.

Reverend Nelson Davis was mentioned as helping a runaway reach Bedford. Nelson was recorded on the 1850 Bedford Township census as a 32-year-old black man, born in Maryland. Nelson was married to Mariah Cooper, who was born an enslaved person in 1815. Mariah's enslaver expressed a desire to free enslaved people upon his death. The son of the enslaver decided to sell Mariah's husband before his father's demise. While her husband was taken to an auction, Mariah's half-sister, a white woman, helped Mariah escape. Nelson and Mariah lived in an area of Bedford known today as Meadowbrook Terrace. One son, DeCharmes Davis, was a well thought of Bedford County veteran of the Civil War. DeCharmes was 16 years old when he volunteered in the 32nd U.S.C.T. His son, Richard, was one of the first three black students to graduate from Bedford High School in 1895. [7]

DeCharmes Davis posing for a Civil War Veterans photograph at the courthouse in 1915. (B.C.H.S)

Wyatt Perry helped runaways reach the home of Harry Marshall in Bedford Township. Harry Marshall was described on census records as a mulatto man born in Maryland about 1790. His wife Nancy was born in Maryland around 1805. The first of their eight children were born in 1830. The 1850 Bedford Township census listed Harry Marshall as a laborer who owned the property the family lived on.

Wyatt helped a boy from Frostburg, MD, reach Rev. John Fidler in Bedford. Fidler was a well-known agent of the Underground Railroad. According to census records, Fidler was born in Virginia. The following obituary was published in the Everett Press on October 2nd, 1891. It paints a picture of an extraordinary man.

> Rev. John Fidler died at the residence of his son-in-law, Isaac Gorden, in Everett on Sunday September 27th, at 12 ½ o'clock, aged about 92 years, having been born on October 10, 1799. John Fidler came to Bedford in 1830 from Ohio and worked at the Bedford House, then kept by Mr. Reynolds. In 1842 he embraced religion on Walnut Hill while on his way from Bedford to the Spring at night. He felt as he was walking along the power of the spirit and fell down on his knees and prayed until he realized that his sins were forgiven and that he was born again. Six months later, he was made a local deacon in the A. M. E. Zion church and began to preach at once. He established a church in conjunction with a minister at Bedford and built the little church on the hill above the limestone quarry, in which the members of the church worshipped for forty years and which about five years ago was abandoned about as a house of worship. He continued to preach in Bedford till '72 when he was an ordained elder. His wife died soon after and he joined the itinerary and preached in different parts of this state and Ohio, for four years, when he became disabled by a fall and returned to Bedford and for several years, till 1883, he filled vacancies when not being able to continue his work, he came to Everett and made his home with Mr. Gordon where he remained till his death.
>
> Mr. Fidler was a man of strong constitution and great endurance. He had great influence with the members of his church and, in fact, with all the colored people of Bedford. His opin-

ion and advice was law to them. For forty years, he was their leader, and no man ever had a more faithful following. Mr. Fidler was the leader of the Underground railroad and hundreds of colored people, probably more than a thousand, were helped on their way to freedom through him. He was assisted by Henry Barks, who is still living and others, but it was Fldler's brain that did the planning. Later, when the slave was freed and the right to vote was given the colored men, he was an ardent and uncompromising Republican and there was little voting for Democrats by the colored men while he was in Bedford. He was a man of strong character, possessed ability of a high order and had all the characteristics of a leader. His life, after embracing religion, was correct and upright and he never backslid. Rev. Fidler was not only honored and loved by his people but was highly respected and enjoyed the confidence of the white people of the community. His life was a grand success, and he has left his impress upon the people with whom he lived. He is gone, but his works do follow him. [8]

John Fidler lived in a house on 114 W. John Street in Bedford. The current house shown in this photo replaced the house Fidler owned.

The James Parson slave catcher story cited by Wyatt Petty is well documented. Jacob Green fled slavery in Romney, West Virginia in 1855. An Altoona Tribune article, published on April 12th, 1883, described the attempted apprehension of Jacob Green in Hollidaysburg. The following is a transcript of the article.

> Our Hollidaysburg correspondent sends us the following: In the good old days before the war, Hollidaysburg was an important station on the "Underground Railroad," and many a fugitive slave received kindly aid and assistance on his journey toward Canada and freedom. Sometime during the summer of 1855, nearly twenty-eight years ago, a Virginian named Parsons came to Hollidaysburg in search of a slave named Green, whom he had tracked to this place. After several days' search, during which Green remained in hiding, the latter attempted to leave on the train. Parsons, however, was on the same train and Green, on discovering this fact, leaped from the car closely followed by Parsons, who gave vigorous chase and collared his victim, attempting to take him along without further ceremony. This occurred in the borough of Gaysport (a section of Hollidaysburg) and was witnessed by a number of citizens, one of whom was General Potts, afterward mayor of Altoona, The general, though a democrat, was a law-abiding citizen and not relishing the Virginian's abrupt way of doing business he at once collared Parsons, and now the row begun in earnest. Major Jesse R. Crawford, also a democrat, who still resides in Gaysport, and who a friend and neighbor of General Potts, relates that he came on the scene at this time, and heard Potts say, "We have laws here, and you must proceed according to law. I will go with you before a justice where you can prove your property." To this Parsons replied by damning Pennsylvania and Pennsylvania laws, declaring that the negro was his, and he was going to take him. General Potts was not a man to be bluffed in this manner, and the discussion was at fever heat in a moment. Parsons soon attempted to end the controversy by trying to draw a pistol on his adversary, but was baffled by Major Crawford, who caught his arm and impressively warned him that a resort to such extreme measures would not do in this country. He then returned the weapon to his pocket. Meanwhile, the friends and sympathizers of the fugitive were not idle. In a surprisingly short time, Parsons and his friends found themselves surrounded by an angry, unfriendly crowd, noisy, turbulent, and rapidly developing a good-sized riot. They had begun to assemble at the first, and the delay occasioned by the altercation with Messrs. Potts and Crawford was improved to the utmost by the negro's friends. At the moment when

Parsons found himself defeated in his pistol practice, Snyder Carr, a colored barber, caught hold of the man Green and dragged him from the grasp of Parsons. Several other bystanders speedily closed in after the slave, the rest of the crowd running hither and thither in the greatest excitement and confusion, and thus succeeded in the object of throwing the pursuers off the track of the fugitive. The negro Green, after an exciting chase, was finally taken to Chimney ridge, south of town, where he remained until nightfall. He was then conducted to Brush Mountain, and from thence was piloted along by-ways and bridle-paths west of the Alleghenies, where he remained hid for several weeks before resuming his journey to Canada. When Parsons found that his victim had escaped, he instituted a suit against General Potts for resisting the action of the "Fugitive Slave Law." The general came up smiling, promptly gave bail for his appearance at court, and had a warrant issued against Parsons on a charge of kidnapping. The trial came before the October term of court in 1855. J. Randolph Tucker, of Virginia, who came to represent Parsons, on learning how badly his client had acted was glad, on account of some informality in the indictment, to avail himself of a motion to quash, which was done. This ended the affair, so far as it related to this county, but it attracted the widest attention throughout the country and there is no doubt that it aided greatly in promoting the bitterness that was already developing between the north and south. [9]

Additional information on the Jacob Green story was found on the Blairsville PA Underground Railroad website. A man by the name of George W. Stump was likely the enslaver of Jacob Green and possibly one of the unnamed "friends" of James Parsons, who were surrounded by the mob in Hollidaysburg. [10] Stump was the nephew of James "Big Jim" Parsons. Both lived in Romney, West Virginia. During the Civil War, Stump was a captain in the 18th Virginia Cavalry and served under General John D. Imboden. Imboden's Confederate Cavalry units clashed many times with Bedford County soldiers during the war. Stump was killed at his father's house near Romney by Union Soldiers in 1865, two months before the war ended. [11]

Portrait of George W. Stump.(Stump family tree on Ancestry.com)

Wyatt Perry likely witnessed and possibly took part in helping Jacob Green escape in Hollidaysburg. The last story cited in the letter was Wyatt Perry serving as a conductor for 9 members of the Mitchel family. Wyatt guided the family through Cumberland Valley to Henry Barks in Bedford. After these actions were discovered, Wyatt was threatened and the family abruptly left Bedford County. A record of Wyatt's daughter, Corilla, being born in Hollidaysburg on January 2nd, 1855, confirms the story. [12]

Henry Barks was born near Sharpsburg, MD around 1812 to a white father and black mother. He was raised as a free black child by Jacob and Anna Strohmenger, a white family in Cumberland Valley. [13] Henry's son, William Tecumseh Barks, volunteered in the 54th Massachusetts, one of the first black regiments of the Civil War. After the war, William became a prominent leader in the black community in Pittsburgh, a published writer, and a celebrated poet. [14] The granddaughters of Henry Barks, Carrie and Susan Barks, were two of the first three black students to graduate from Bedford High School in 1895. [15]

Not all stories during this era were noble acts of helping enslaved people gain freedom. A despicable kidnapping of a black child in Cumberland Valley was published in a Bedford Inquirer on November 2nd, 1860. The following is a transcript of what was reported in the article.

> An atrocious act of kidnapping was committed in Cumberland Valley, about six miles south of Bedford, on Thursday last. Two little girls, about six years old, children of George Love, a respectable colored man, were playing almost within sight of the house, when a man rushed out of the woods, snatched up one of the children and ran away with her. The other child hastened home and gave the alarm, hut there were, unfortunately, no man about the bouse at the time, and the kidnapper thus got a fair start with his victim. It is evident that the villain,

whoever he is, was well acquainted with the premises and the habits of its occupants. It is believed that the child was carried to Maryland and sold into slavery. The parents were liberated about ten years ago by a humane Virginia master, who, besides granting them freedom, gave them means to buy the land upon which they live, which they have been cultivating ever since with care and industry. They are greatly distressed about their stolen child, but we earnestly hope that she will yet be recovered. We also hope the villainous perpetrator of the deed may be discovered and compelled to do the State service in the penitentiary. Hanging is too good for the mercenary wretch. The kidnappers have heretofore driven a good trade in catching fugitive slaves, but as that article of commerce has become somewhat scarce of late, owing to the vigilance of the masters, they are now trying their hands at stealing free children. [16]

This story had a good ending. A week later, the Bedford Inquirer reported the kidnapper, William Hemming, had been arrested, and the child had been returned safely to the parents. Hemming, a Cumberland Valley resident, took the child to the Cumberland Maryland jail and claimed the little girl was the daughter of an enslaved woman who had not yet been captured. The scheme included a second man who claimed ownership of the little girl and the mother. [17] George Love was part of the group of former Carter plantation enslaved people freed twenty years earlier.

A Bedford Inquirer article was written in 1950, provides additional details on the kidnapping. The name of the little girl was Delilah. Bedford District Attorney George Spang contacted the Sheriff of Allegany County, MD. and learned a badly frightened little black girl was dropped off by a slave catcher at the Cumberland Maryland Jail. Spang judged it unsafe for a black man to travel south of the state line. James Brown, a white neighbor of Delilah's uncle, John Love, knew the girl and volunteered to bring her back to Bedford County. William Hemming stood trial for kidnapping. The following is an excerpt on his acquittal in the 1950 article.

> For some reasons the case was twice continued, until September 1861 when he was tried by jury, which returned a verdict of "not guilty for want of sufficient evidence," and discharged, owing, without doubt, to political conditions of the time. Within a month, he enlisted in the armed services.

William Hemming enlisted in the 2nd PA Cavalry in November 1861. After the war, census records show he lived in Allegany County, MD, and died there in 1892. James Brown, the white neighbor who brought Delilah back home from Cumberland, was a Civil War veteran. James enlisted in the 22nd PA Cavalry in February 1864 and returned home to Bedford after the war ended. He passed in 1874. George Love also served in the Union Army. No details were found on his U.S.C.T. enlistment or any other information on his life after the war. John Love, George's brother, served in the 41st U.S.C.T. regiment. A story of John Love serving as an underground railroad conductor is in chapter 13 - Bedford. Delilah Love died a tragic death. In 1914, while ironing, she accidentally overturned a lamp, causing a fire. She died hours later. [18]

Being kidnapped and sold into slavery was feared in many black communities in Pennsylvania. A local historian estimated upwards of 50 black children in Philadelphia were being seized each year in the 1820s. The 1826 Pennsylvania Personal Liberty Law was enacted, making it illegal to capture or entice free black people from Pennsylvania to be enslaved. [19] Unfortunately, the law did not stop free blacks from being kidnapped and sold into slavery.

Information about an elected official from Bedford County being accused of kidnapping a black woman and her child was found. On November 11th, 1835, the Hagerstown Torch Light newspaper reported two men from Bedford County, Thomas R. Gettys and George Raum, were arrested by constables in Hagerstown. Both were charged with kidnapping a black woman named Ellen Colbreth and a child named George Brown. [20]

The following week, the Adams Sentinel in Gettysburg published an article with additional details on the kidnapping. The article listed the names of the accused men as Thomas R. Gettys and Conrad Rohm and the kidnapped woman as Ellen Galbraith. Galbraith and her child, George Brown, were abducted in Bedford and taken to Hagerstown to be sold into slavery. The article indicates the reason for the crime was to get the woman and the illegitimate child of one captor out of Bedford County. [21] No other information was found on whether Gettys or Rohm ever faced trial. Nor is it known which man may have been the father of the child. Records show both men were married and had children prior to the kidnapping.

Thomas R. Gettys was born in 1787. He served as the Bedford County Treasurer from 1815 to 1818 and a second term from 1829 to 1831. Gettys was the founder and publisher of The True American, an early newspaper in Bedford. The newspaper was in print from 1813 until 1824. In 1827, Gettys founded the Democratic Inquirer in Bedford. He served as the publisher for five or six years. He was a onetime Democrat candidate for the State Senate and was commissioned as a Justice of the Peace in Bedford in 1820. His obituary stated he was the first County Superintendent of Public Schools. Gettys died in 1860 in Bedford. [22] Conrad Rohm was born in 1796 in Fayette County. He was listed on the 1820 Washington County (Hagerstown) census, the Bedford County census reports in 1840 and 1850, and on the 1860 census report in Allegheny County, Maryland. Little else was found on Rohm. [23] No information was found on Ellen Galbraith or George Brown.

Another kidnapping of a free black man seized in Fulton County was reported in the Pittsburgh Post in 1851. Charles Wedley, a free black man in Pittsburgh, was induced to travel to Philadelphia. A white man named Speer and a black man, Lindsay Lewis, offered to pay his way. All three set out on foot together, presumably on the Lincoln Highway–Route 30. When they reached Licking Creek, a group of ruffians seized Wedley and claimed they knew he escaped from Wheeling. Newspaper articles listed Licking Creek as being in Bedford County. In 1850, Licking Creek Township became part of the newly formed Fulton County. Wedley was placed in irons and taken across the Maryland line by the ruffians. Speer and Lindsay Lewis returned to Pittsburgh without visiting Philadelphia. Upon arriving in Pittsburgh, they told the aunt of Wedley he was in Philadelphia.

Wedley was offered for sale to a man in Maryland who was acquainted with the city of Pittsburgh. Wedley entered into a long conversation with the would-be enslaver who became convinced Wedley was a free black. The man told the captors he wouldn't buy Wedley at any price and the captors took Wedley away and chained him to a bedpost. The next day, the would-be enslaver went to where Wedley was being held and helped him escape from his captors. Wedley arrived back in Pittsburgh two weeks after initially leaving the city.

Wedley was listed on the 1840 Pittsburgh census as living with seven other free blacks. No other information on Wedley was found. The men who lured him out of Pittsburgh were arrested. No further information was found on a trial or conviction. Lindsay Lewis was listed on the 1850 Allegheny (Pittsburg) census as a 27-year-old mulatto working as a boatman. This census record noted Lewis had a previous larceny conviction. No other information was found on Lewis, Speer, or the ruffians that seized Wedley in Licking Creek Township. The identity of the man who helped free Wedley is unknown. [24]

William Lloyd Garrison's abolitionist newspaper, The Liberator, repeatedly warned about some free blacks turning in enslaved blacks for a reward. On August 29th, 1856, the Liberator reported free blacks in Washington, Pennsylvania (near Pittsburgh) tarred and feathered a black man for aiding in the capture of enslaved people. [25] No other details were mentioned in this brief article. Nimrod Warren, who was part of the group of the enslaved people on the Carter plantation, reportedly knew of a black man who turned in enslaved people for a share of the reward. Howard Cessna responded to a request for information from Wilbur Siebert in 1944. The following is a verbatim excerpt from this letter.

Old Nimrod Warren, who used to work for my grandfather, said the colored citizen who took

> Two men from Bedford county, named Thomas R. Gettys and Conrad Rohm, were arrested at Hagerstown last week, and committed to prison, on the charge of kidnapping a free black woman named Ellen Galbraith and child, and a negro boy named George Brown. They were taken from Bedford, and offered for sale in Hagerstown. The Bedford Gazette says, "there are many circumstances connected with this nefarious outrage, which we forbear to publish, because the affair will shortly become the subject of judicial scrutiny. and we sincerely hope that that scrutiny may be *strict, piercing, stern* and *inflexible.*" The same paper also intimates, that "this glaring violation of the laws was superinduced by something more than a mere desire to make money out of the flesh and blood of a fellow-creature. A question as to the *paternity* of the child is about to undergo a judicial investigation, and this may account for an anxiety amongst some persons to get the woman out of the county." This adds to the heinousness of the offence against the law.

Published in the Adams Sentinel, Gettysburg on November 16th, 1835. (Newspapers.com)

charge of the runaways, sometimes would turn (them) over to the owner and with the money build a house here in Bedford, the sight of which always made Nimrod mad. [26]

Underground Railroad research suggests it was not common, but not unheard of, for free blacks to turn in enslaved people for a share of a reward. [27] Nimrod was born in 1841. His parents, Nathan and Julia, gained their freedom on the Thomas O.B. Carter plantation in Fauquier County, Virginia, around the time Nimrod was born. The 1850 and 1860 Cumberland Valley census records listed Nimrod and his family living on the Bear Track Station property, referenced in the Wyatt Perry letter. Nimrod volunteered in the 43rd U.S.C.T. regiment during the Civil War. He survived the Battle of the Crater near Petersburg in 1864 and mustered out of the Union Army after the war ended. Nimrod was the father of six children and passed in 1917.

> ☞ A negro has been tarred and feathered, by his colored brethren, at Washington, Pa., in consequence of it being clearly proved that he was in the employ of slaveholders, in hunting up fugitives.

Notice in "The Liberator" abolitionist newspaper on August 29th, 1856.
(fair-use.org)

Chapter 13

Bedford

John W. Rouse, a 49-year-old black attorney in Bedford, initially responded to a request for information from Wilbur H. Siebert on November 25th, 1895. The following is a verbatim transcription of the first extraordinary letter sent to Siebert on the Underground Railroad era.

> Abraham Barnhart, Mayor of Bedford, Pa., handed me a letter requesting me to give you some data of the working of the underground railroad in Bedford County, Pennsylvania. I am the only son of Rev. Elias Rouse, one of the active members of the said organization, my father having died April 10th, 1892, and by marriage I am a relative of Joseph Crawley and Rev. John Fidler, the other two members of the said organization of Bedford, PA. I have personal recollection of John Brown, in 1859, he was at my father's house and associated with my father and my father-in-law and my wife's uncle Rev. John Fidler. I was a small boy in 1858 or 1859 and have personal knowledge of my father starting with slaves in Bedford, Pa., eighteen miles north to a town in Bedford County, named Pleasantville, known as a Quaker settlement to the house of a Quaker by the name of Benjamin H. Walker, they would be put on a hay wagon and hay thrown on them and they were hauled to Blair County, Pa., and put in case of William Nesbit, Esq. of Altoona, Pa., who died a few weeks ago. He was one of the active members of the organization. I have personal recollections of my father going away after night with fugitive slaves, and he would be gone for days and they would keep the man concealed at day and travel at night. My only recollection of this was in 1858-1859.

> I have a faint recollection of a test case of the Fugitive Slave Law in Bedford County. A writ of habeas corpus and a prisoner were brought before Associate Judge John Hartley, who is now living in Bedford, PA., and is a wealthy banker. The runaway had got two or three miles east of Bedford, when a member of that class of people who would not work, started after the runaway slave and he was caught and about to be taken to his master, when said member of the underground railroad had the body of this runaway brought before his Honor. The attorneys were: Joseph Tate, Esq., for the master and Hon. Geo. H. Spang for the Underground Railroad; after a full hearing, Judge Hartley discharged the prisoner. This is a copy of the death notice of Elias Rouse, copied from the Bedford Inquirer on April 15, 1892, published in Bedford, Pennsylvania.

> Elias Rouse, the well-known colored barber of Bedford, Pa., died on Sunday morning last after a lingering illness of several years. He was born in Cumberland Valley, July 22, 1822. His life was comparatively uneventful until after the beginning of anti-slavery agitation after the passage of the Fugitive Slave Law. Mr. Rouse became one of the active engineers of the underground railroad, an organization for assisting fugitive slaves to reach Canada. The organization was very active in giving information and furnishing hiding places and guides and in every way possible to assist fugitives to reach the Canadian Border. John Fidler and Joseph Crawley were also members of the organization. Mr. Rouse was the last of this colored band, who risked their lives and liberties in order to assist their colored brothers to escape from slavery.

> In 1859, John Brown visited Bedford and was for several days a guest of Mr. Rouse, while arranging for the Harper's Ferry Insurrection. Rouse, Joseph Crawley and John Fidler, and

some others were engaged in recruiting for Brown, but the extent of their labor and the number of their recruits will probably never be known. After Brown's capture, Rouse fled to London, Canada, where he had relatives, and did not return until about the time of the breaking out of the rebellion. Since then, he has resided here and quietly pursued his humble calling. He early became a member of the A.M.E. Church. He was a preacher among his colored brethren for a number of years and purchased the ground and erected the Bethel A.M.E. Church on Gravel Hill at his own expense. If you want any more, write me. [1]

Several significant historical events are cited in the letter. John H. Rouse confirmed John Brown met with his father, Elias Rouse, Joseph Crawley, and John Fidler four months prior to the ill-fated Harpers Ferry raid. Elias Rouse fled to Canada after John Brown was captured. This act demonstrated considerable concern by Rouse for being implicated as a Brown accomplice. The story of John Brown and his visit to Bedford County in June 1859 is covered in chapter 14 of this book.

John H. Rouse acknowledged his father served as a conductor for enslaved people. Elias Rouse traveled at night with enslaved people to reach the home of Benjamin H. Walker near Pleasantville. The letter noted Walker transported freedom seekers in hay wagons to William Nesbit in Blair County, PA. Walker is also cited for transporting runaways to Cambria County in other documents. Having choices in safe houses helped in the evasion of pursuing slave catchers.

The letter contained the Bedford Inquirer obituary of Elias Rouse, stating he became active in the Underground Railroad when the Fugitive Slave Act passed in 1850. The following is a transcript of a second obituary published in the Bedford Gazette.

On Sunday morning, one of the oldest and best-known colored men of Bedford, Eli Rouse, died at his home on Pitt Street, of congestion of the brain. Mr. Rouse was born in Cumberland Valley, July 23, 1822, and was therefore in his 70th year. He has always lived in Bedford except when he was in Philadelphia learning his trade, that of a barber. He commenced to barber in this place in 1840 and followed that occupation ever since. For several years, he was a minister of the gospel, and in 1868 built the Bethel church at his own expense. He joined the church when but thirteen or fourteen years of age. The deceased was the uncle of George W. Williams, the famous colored historian who was appointed minister to Haiti during President Arthur's administration. Mr. Williams died six months ago in Europe, while returning from Africa. He was a frequent visitor to the Springs and was born in a house which used to stand near the spring by the iron bridge on the road leading across the mountain. [2]

Both Rouse and Joseph Crawley were well-known local barbers. Barber shops were social gathering places. Communications with members of the community helped coordinate Underground Railroad activities. Limited information is available on Joseph Crawley. He was born in Maryland in 1819 and passed in 1873. No newspaper editions containing Joseph Crawley's obituary have been located. Crawley is buried in the Old Presbyterian Cemetery in Bedford.

Elias Rouse, Joseph Crawley, and John Fidler were closely associated with the A.M.E. Church in Bedford. John Fidler was the long-time pastor, and Elias Rouse also served as a preacher during his lifetime. They likely exchanged Underground Railroad communications with fellow A.M.E. preacher, Thomas Henry. Henry was a long-time saddlebag preacher with stints in the Hollidaysburg and Cumberland Maryland circuits. [3] A.M.E. preachers also attended regional church conferences. Thomas Henry undoubtably would have known John Fidler, and likely knew Elias Rouse and Joseph Crawley. The names of all four men were found in the papers of John Brown after the Harpers Ferry raid in 1859. No documentation directly linking Henry with Fidler, Rouse, or Crawley has been found. An overview of Thomas Henry is provided in chapter 9 – Cumberland Maryland.

In the letter, John H. Rouse mentioned a vague recollection of a Habeas Corpus case involving a runaway captured two to three miles east of Bedford. Joseph Tate, attorney for the enslaver, George H. Spang attorney for the Underground Railroad, and Judge John G. Hartley, who heard the case, were familiar names in local legal circles. No information was found on this court case. Spang began practicing law in Bedford on May 3, 1854, which places the hearing after that date. [4] Documentation exists of Judge Hartley's home, a stone house near Lower Snake Spring Road, being an Underground Railroad station. [5] Apprehension of the enslaved person would have taken place about 3 miles from Hartley's home. Therefore, Judge Hartley, deciding to set the freedom seeker free, is not surprising.

An interesting aspect of this story is the father of John G. Hartley was a term enslaver. William Hartley II registered Nancy Smith as a servant until age 28. From 1817 until 1825, three of Nancy Smith's children, Mary, a male child named Smith, and Isaac, were also registered as servants until age 28. Ambiguous text in the Pennsylvania Gradual Abolition Act of 1780 interpreted the children born to term enslaved people could also be registered as servants for 28 years. More information on this issue is contained in chapter 4 - Fugitive Slave Legislation. [6] The 1830 census recorded five free blacks living at the Hartley residence. There were two boys under 10, one girl aged 10 to 23, one woman aged 24 to 35, and a woman over 55. No further details were found on Nancy Smith, her children, or when they gained their freedom. William Hartley II died in 1837. No references to enslaved people were found in his will. The 1840 census for Catherine Hartley, the widow of William Hartley II, recorded 4 free blacks living at the residence. One male under 10, two males from 10 to 23, and 1 male age 24 to 35 were listed. The 1850 census for John G. Hartley listed no blacks residing on the property.

John G. Hartley was profiled in a biographical book of the leading citizens of Bedford and Somerset Counties. Judge Hartley was described as an exemplary husband and father, a kind neighbor and a public-spirited citizen who enjoyed the sincere respect of the community. Both he and his wife were active members of the Methodist Episcopal church in Snake Spring Valley. As with the Barndollars in Bloody Run, the Methodist Church stance on slavery may have shaped the differing views on slavery of John G. Hartley and his father. [7]

William Hartley house east of Everett on Route 30.

Registration of Nancy Smith and a child named Mary by William Hartley in 1817. (Pennsylvania Historical and Museum Commission)

Elias Rouse, Joseph Crawley, and John Fidler coordinated much of the Underground Railroad activity around Bedford. Many others served as conductors and safe house station operators in and near Bedford. John Love was mentioned as the person who provided sanctuary to a group of six freedom seekers in a newspaper article published in 1936. The following is a transcription of a newspaper article titled, "Nancy Watkins Recalls Oppressing Days of Slavery."

> Of interest to local people is the following interesting sketch of Mrs. Nancy Green Watkins, a former resident of Everett. The article appeared in the "Today and Yesterday" column of the Johnstown Tribune:
>
> Harking back to the days of Slavery is the story of the escape from a Maryland plantation of a little group of oppression-weary people who had for a long time dreamed of the day when they could slip across the border into Pennsylvania, a free State. More than 75 years have passed and the hardships and terror of the flight, by darkness, from the grim life of serfdom are but a memory today for one of the younger members of the band, Mrs. Nancy Green

Watkins of Bedford, who last month reached her 91st birthday.

Mrs. Watkins was in her teens when she last saw the plantation. She has forgotten many of the details of the long walk that brought them into Bedford County and safety, but the desperation and fear that spurred them on did not fail to leave an indelible impression in her mind. She recalls, vaguely, the furtive planning for the escape after one of the older women, Mehalla Craig, had fallen into the bad graces of her mistress and was to be flogged the next day. In flashes of reminiscence there comes back the picture of how they started under the cover of darkness her father, younger brother, and sister, Mehalla Craig, and Nancy Streets, (Aunt Nancy to the motherless children). Mrs. Watkins' mother had died some years earlier. On through the night they walked, the father carrying the younger children most of the distance, 'til by daybreak they had left the Sam Brady plantation and its drudgery some miles behind. Constant fear of pursuit, she says, caused them to be wary and to "lay low" until darkness again made it safer for them to be on the road. And thus it was until they finally reached Bedford, exhausted and hungry, and found sanctuary at the home of another former slave, John Love. The pursuit they feared did materialize but all in vain, for the plantation foreman sent to Bedford after them was forced to return empty-handed.

Mrs. Watkins' father was Jackson Green, who had been sold to Sam Brady, the plantation owner in Cumberland County, Maryland, for a paltry sum. On the plantation, Jackson Green saw his family increase, and the children initiated into the lives of slaves by the assignment to them of light duties. Housed on the plantation were upwards of 40 slaves, Mrs. Watkins recalls, and their task was not a light one, what with hundreds of acres under cultivation, a grist mill and a distillery requiring attention.

It is a matter of pride with Mrs. Watkins and her children that her father did not waste a day in securing employment once they were in free territory. The day after their arrival in Bedford, she recalls, he entered the service of George Anderson and remained with him a number of years before going to Colorado. He returned to Bedford and passed his last years there. He died at the age of 102 and his ability to walk from Bedford to Everett when over 100 years old is still talked about.

Mrs. Watkins looks back with some regret to the fact that she never had a single day of schooling and was so far as she can remember, never inside a school. This handicap did not prevent her learning to spell and to read a little. She attributes her long life to the fact that she has always worked hard and lived simply and righteously. Today she is a well-preserved woman. Her husband, Hiram Watkins, served in the Union Army in the Civil War and later was a layman missionary in Haiti. He died in Everett at the age of 93. Mrs. Watkins, long a member of the A. M. E. Church in Everett, recently left that town to make her home with her daughter, Mrs. Orange Gordon, of Bedford. A son, William Watkins. lives in Huntingdon. [8]

Nancy Green Watkins passed away in February 1937, the year after this article was published. Her husband, Hiram, was listed on the 1890 Everett Veterans Census. He volunteered in the 26th U.S.C.T. regiment in February 1864 and returned home after the Civil War ended. Hiram passed away in 1917. Jackson Green, the father of Nancy, lived until 1908. Nancy, Hiram, and Jackson are buried in the Everett Cemetery. The 1870 Bedford Census listed Nancy Streets as a 70-year-old housekeeper living with Jackson Green and his wife, Eliza. No information was found on Nancy's brother and sister or Mehalla Craig. [9]

John Love was born into slavery on the Thomas O. B. Carter Plantation in Virginia in 1811. When Carter died in 1840, John Love and the other members of his family were set free. The Love family and many other enslaved people on the Carter Plantation settled in Bedford County. John Love, his wife and small child were recorded on the 1860 Bedford Township census. He was listed as a laborer who owned his home. John Love volunteered in the 41st U.S.C.T. on September 21st, 1864, and returned home when the war ended. John passed in 1907 and is buried in the Eastern Lights Cemetery in Altoona. [10]

The article mentioned another man who helped the freedom seekers. George Anderson hired Jackson Green the day after he arrived in Bedford. George W. Anderson was a well-known doctor who owned a sizable property on the eastern side of Bedford. The 1860 census listed the value of his real estate at $20,000, a tidy sum in that era. Being a highly educated man, it seems unlikely Anderson would not have figured out Jackson Green was an escaped slave. Anderson died in 1879 at age 70. The following biography excerpts offer some insights into the character of George Anderson.

> George W. Anderson was a most excellent type of the old-time gentleman, always courteous and considerate of the feelings of others. In his dealings, he was scrupulously honest, and his liberality was proverbial. Except for his intimate friends, he was uniformly reticent, but he had a warm, sympathetic heart, and those who saw him only on the surface little suspected the deep undercurrent of kind feeling, warm attachment and general solicitude which were the salient points in his character. [11]

George W. Anderson's father was Dr. John Anderson, founder of the Bedford Springs Hotel. John Anderson was also a term enslaver. He registered two enslaved people in 1822. Mary and her six-month-old daughter Sophia were claimed as servants until age 28. The 1830 census listed one free black male and one free black female both in the 24 to 34 age range, and a free black female under the age of 10 living at the Anderson residence. Dr. John Anderson died in 1840. [12] A genealogy book referenced John Anderson having seven male enslaved people on his property. The following is the excerpt from the book.

Dr. George W. Anderson.
(History of Bedford, Somerset and Fulton Counties)

> When John Anderson's wife died, and his daughters moved to Pittsburgh, he kept house with seven male slaves, and had no women in the house. On his death, he freed all his slaves and gave to each a cabin of logs with an acre of ground on the mountain side. [13]

John Anderson's wife died in 1815. The seven male enslaved people mentioned in the genealogy book are at odds with census records and term registration records of two female servants. No other information is known about Mary, her daughter Sophia, or the seven male enslaved people. No references were found on the differences between George W. Anderson and his father on slavery. The Anderson's were Presbyterians. In 1818, the Presbyterian church declared the system "inconsistent with the law of God and totally irreconcilable with the gospel of Christ". The following is an excerpt from a book published in 1898 on the Underground Railroad.

> A sect to which a considerable proportion of underground operators belonged was Calvinistic in its creed. All the various wings of Presbyterianism seem to have had representatives in this class of anti-slavery people. The sinfulness of slavery was a proposition that found uncompromising advocates among the Presbyterian ministers of the South in the early part of the 19th century. [14]

Dr. John Anderson.
(Hickhok Genealogy Book)

The following is an excerpt from a Presbyterian church resolution in 1818.

> In 1818, the denomination's General Assembly (the successor to the Synod), adopted a resolution. We consider the voluntary enslaving of one part of the human race by another as a gross violation of the most precious and sacred rights of human nature and utterly inconsistent with the law of God. The Assembly called on all Christians "as speedily as possible to efface this blot on our holy religion" and "to obtain the complete abolition of slavery

The Dr. George W. Anderson house once stood near the cross streets of Anderson and East Pitt Street along the Juniata River. (Hickhok Genealogy Book)

Drawing of Dr. George W. Anderson's house and wire bridge over the Juniata River. (1853 Bedford Map by Thomas Doran)

throughout Christendom." The resolution passed unanimously. [15]

Another prominent Bedford resident cited as being an Underground Railroad agent whose parents were term enslavers was Major John Watson. A historic Bedford house known as "the Grove" is referenced in two books written on the Underground Railroad. [16] Lt. Colonel Hugh Barclay served as a Deputy Quartermaster during the Revolutionary War. After the war, he received a warrant for a 400-acre property adjoining the town of Bedford. Hugh Barclay built "the Grove" house, also referred to as "Poplar Grove" around 1794. Barclay passed in 1807. He is buried in the Old Presbyterian Graveyard. [17] The Grove property was sold to Dr. John Anderson in 1808. Anderson resold the property to Dr. William Watson shortly after his marriage to Eliza Hartley in 1811. [18] Watson was born in Mifflin County, Pennsylvania, in 1779 and moved to Bedford County in 1809.

Records show Dr. William Watson registered a female servant named Rachel Jameson. From 1815 until 1823, Rachel gave birth to five children: Henry, Sophia, Sarah, Charles, and Jeremiah. All were registered as being servants until age 28. [19] No further information was found on Rachel, her children or when they

Chapter 13 - Bedford   69

Pre-Civil War era drawing of the Major John Watson "Grove" house. (Hickhok Genealogy Book)

An 1853 Map of Bedford shows Major John Watson and Dr. George W. Anderson owned large neighboring properties that appear uninhabited except for the Watson and Anderson houses. The Watson property included areas east of S. Juliana Street and south of E. John Street to Shobers Run. Anderson's bordering property would have extended to areas east of East Street to near where East Pitt and East Penn streets meet. The Bedford County Historical Society has an original copy of the 1853 Bedford Map by Thomas Doran showing the Watson and Anderson properties.

The "Grove" house on Grove Lane in Bedford.

gained their freedom. William Watson died in 1835. His son, Major John Watson, lived on the "Grove" property with his mother until his death in 1862. John Watson died in Philadelphia. There are no records showing he was enlisted in the Civil War at the time of his death. [20] Major John Watson and Dr. George W. Anderson owned large neighboring properties on the eastern side of Bedford according to an 1853 map of the town. The 1850 census records show John Watson was a neighbor to Henry Marshall. Henry Marshall was cited as being an Underground Railroad agent in the Wyatt Perry letter in chapter 12 - Cumberland Valley.

A number of other blacks who lived in Bedford have been documented as Underground Railroad agents. James Graham was born a free black in Shippensburg, Pennsylvania, in 1825. James and his wife, Mary Cosler Graham, were listed as Bedford Borough residents in the 1850 census. The 1860 census recorded the Graham's owned farmland in Bedford Township and were the parents of 6 children. James hid enslaved people in hay and tree fruit wagons in route to markets in Somerset and Johnstown. [21] James may have transported freedom seekers to well-known agent George Cobaugh, who operated a station on his farm near Somerset. The Cobaugh family suffered a tragedy during the Civil War. George's son, John Cobaugh,

Photograph of George Cobaugh. Bedford County conductor James Graham likely transported freedom seekers to the Underground Railroad station on the George Cobaugh farm near Somerset. (Cobaugh family tree on Ancestry.com)

Four Generation photograph of the James Graham family. Wife Mary Cosler Graham is seated. On her left is daughter, Elizabeth; on the right is granddaughter Margaret and on Mary's lap is great-grandson Nini. (Pittsburgh Post-Gazette black history article - December 17th, 1995)

suffered a severe wound at the battle of the Wilderness in May 1864. He died two weeks later after his right leg was amputated. [22]

Annie Gilchrist, a longtime editor of the Bedford Inquirer, wrote an article, "Our Colored Friends" in 1950. The following is an excerpt from the article.

> Uncle John Harris was a "conductor," escaping slaves from the Cumberland section stopping at his cabin in "Africa" (west of Bedford at the site of the present boro reservoir) for directions and were aided in reaching Punxsutawney, then into Canada and freedom. That section was so named prior to the Civil War. [23]

John Harris was born in Bedford County in 1836 and was a next-door neighbor with fellow Underground Railroad conductor, James Graham. John volunteered in the 3rd U.S.C.T. in July 1863. He survived a face wound suffered on Morris Island, South Carolina, in August or September 1863. He mustered out as a sergeant after the war ended in 1865. John passed in 1914 and is buried in the Mt. Ross Cemetery. [24]

Aaron Young, Jacob Young, and Moses Esrey were proprietors of a butcher shop on the southeast corner of Penn and West Street in Bedford. The butcher shop is identified as a safe house station. [25] Both Aaron and Jacob volunteered in the 24th U.S.C.T. during the Civil War. Another brother, Peter, served in the 127th U.S.C.T. All three brothers survived the war. The Young brothers are buried in the Mt. Ross Cemetery. No information on Moses Esrey was found.

The Civilian and Telegraph newspaper in Cumberland Maryland published an article of an enslaved person escaping in Bedford on August 11, 1859. The story took place while President Buchanan was staying at the Bedford Springs resort.

> We learn from the Pittsburgh Gazette, an incident which transpired at Bedford Springs, during the President's recent visit, will easily bear repeating. In the retinue of President Buchanan - who, according to correspondent of Fourney's Press, was piping and dancing at that watering place - was an accomplished and fashionable Southern widow, who has for several winters occupied a commanding position in the fashionable circles of the national

metropolis. This lady was attended to by a female slave, who, on discovering that she was on the "free soil of a free state," and not having the terrors of the Fugitive Slave Law before her eyes, took French leave of her mistress on Saturday week last, and has not since been heard from. On the discovery of this elopement, the neighboring hills and fastnesses were searched, but the fugitive could not be found. The gallant among whom was P. M. Magraw, of Maryland, returned crestfallen and disappointed. In the meantime, we presume the fugitive is far on her way to Canada via the Underground Railway. [26]

Churches were a center of community life for previous generations. The A.M.E. Zion church was founded around 1845 on Gravel Hill, near the intersection of Penn and West Streets. Many of the Underground Railroad agents listed in this chapter attended services at this church. It is likely other church members provided help to enslaved people. Their names are likely lost to history.

A curious connection to the A.M.E. Zion church involves a white couple, Frederick and Eve Nawgle, who lived in Bedford Township. The Nawgle's deeded the church property for $1.00 in 1855, including the log house where worship was held. [27] A reference from a book written on the Pennsylvania Underground Railroad briefly mentions a Knaugel House in a chapter on Bedford County. The following is the excerpt.

> According to tradition, John Brown, on his way to Harper's Ferry, stayed at the Knaugel House, which was alleged to have been used as an Underground Railroad station. [28]

No other information was found connecting John Brown to a Knaugel House. No individuals with the family name "Knaugel" were found in Bedford County. Frederick and Eve Nawgle were next-door neighbors of John Love, according to the 1860 Bedford Township census. John Love is the conductor cited in the Nancy Green Watkins story in this chapter. The next chapter covers what is known about John Brown's stay in Bedford County in June 1859.

(left) The Young butcher shop property was on the southwest corner of West and Penn streets. The current house shown in this photograph was built after the butcher shop building was dismantled.

(right) 1877 map of Bedford. Red arrows are pointing to the sites of the first A.M.E. Zion church, and the Young Butcher Shop.

(below) The A.M.E. Zion church stood on the hill on the left side of the photograph. The former Harris Hotel, now the Penn West Hotel, is visible on the right.

*Photograph of John Brown in 1859.
(Library of Congress)*

Chapter 14

The Path to Harpers Ferry went through Bedford

The United States was a tinderbox over the issue of slavery in the years prior to the Civil War. A man from Kansas threw a torch on the tinderbox in October 1859. Had John Brown's plan to seize weapons in Harpers Ferry been successful, plantation owners would have faced their worst nightmare - an armed slave uprising. Shortly before the Harpers Ferry raid, John Brown met with three Bedford abolitionists. The following is known about Brown's stay in Bedford and the story of the ill-fated raid, one of the most famous events leading up to the Civil War.

John Brown was born on May 9th, 1800 in Torrington, Connecticut, into a deeply religious family that despised slavery. The family moved to Hudson, Ohio when he was 5 years old. As a young man, Brown planned to attend a seminary, but was dismissed for poor grades at a preparatory school. John Brown married Dianthe Lusk in 1820. Prior to her passing in 1832, Dianthe gave birth to seven children. Brown remarried Mary Anne Day, the year after the death of his first wife. During his life, John Brown worked as a tanner, canal builder, land speculator and sheep farmer. He failed in business several times. [1] Brown moved his family to Springfield, MA in 1846. Here, his path crossed for the first time with Frederick Douglass. Brown was a parishioner in a church where Douglass spoke. [2]

The Kansas-Nebraska Act of 1854 passed over fierce opposition. The legislation created two new states, divided at the 40° parallel. The new law effectively repealed the Missouri Compromise of 1820 that outlawed slavery above the 36°30' parallel. Stephen Douglas, a senator from Illinois, sponsored a "popular sovereignty" amendment to gain the crucial Southern votes needed to pass. [3] Unlike the Missouri Compromise, citizens of each state would decide by popular vote whether Kansas and Nebraska would be free or slave.

Many Northern newspapers portrayed the Kansas territory as a place of natural beauty and fertile soil. After the Kansas-Nebraska Act passed, urgent appeals were made for settlers to save this land of milk and honey from the curse of slavery. Advocates from both sides promoted the settlement of Kansas to citizens sympathetic to their cause. People flooded to Kansas to vote in elections. Soon ballot stuffing, voter intimidation and political shenanigans became common. [4]

Five of John Brown's sons migrated to Kansas in the spring of 1855. John Brown arrived in Osawatomie, Kansas, in October 1855 to join his sons in the free-state cause. [5] Violence erupted in 1856. Terror reigned supreme between pro-slavery "Border Ruffians" from Missouri and free-state "Jayhawkers" in Kansas. Both sides took part in an ugly cycle of murderous raids and retribution killings. John Brown was by far the most well-known anti-slavery figure during this infamous "Bleeding Kansas" era.

The simmering conflict turned to a boil on the night of May 21st, 1856. Several hundred pro-slavery Border Ruffians sacked the abolitionist stronghold of Lawrence, KS. They robbed residents, burned the Free State hotel, and destroyed the printing presses of two newspapers. Three days later, John Brown struck back. Brown, four of his sons, a son-in-law and two other men entered three cabins of pro-slavery settlers. After interrogations, five men were killed with swords or knives. Several were executed by decapitation. Brown spared the lives of some men he didn't believe took part in raids or the killings of free-state settlers. He also spared the lives of the wives and children of the men he killed, even though they could identify him. These killings became known as the Pottawatomie Massacre. [6]

Brown believed he was acting on divine providence. The following were Brown's comments to a friend about Pottawatomie.

> I did not kill them, but I do not pretend to say they were not killed by my order. I believe I was doing God's service. God used me as an instrument to kill those men; and if I live, I think he will use me as an instrument to kill a good many more. I was satisfied each had committed murder in his heart, and according to the Scriptures, they were guilty of murder. I felt justified in having them killed. [7]

After Pottawatomie, Brown recruited a militia. Several pitched battles and skirmishes ensued. The most well-known battle took place on August 30, 1856. Four hundred Border Ruffians swept into Osawatomie and burned the town to the ground. John Brown and 40 outnumbered men attempted to defend the town. Before being driven off, John Brown uttered an apocalyptical maxim. "Take more care to end life well than to live long." His son, Frederick, was killed during the battle. From that time forward, John Brown was widely known as "Osawatomie Brown." [8]

The American public became fascinated by the man whose daring exploits were revered by some and reviled by others. In September 1856, a play "Osawatomie Brown" opened on Broadway. The play assigned blame for the Pottawatomie massacre on pro-slavery interests. Few in the north were fully aware of what happened at Pottawatomie. For abolitionists, John Brown was a symbol of a holy crusade against slavery. Thus, when a fund-raising trip was made to New England in 1857, he wasn't viewed by most as a killer. [9]

Early in 1858, Brown stayed for a month at the home of Frederick Douglass in Rochester, NY. The following are some excerpts of Douglass' observations on Brown.

> John Brown. lean, strong, and sinewy. He was under 6 feet tall with a straight and symmetrical build of less than 150 pounds. His bearing was impressive. Brown walked with a long springing gate. He appeared absorbed by his own reflections, neither seeking nor shunning observation. His eyes were bluish gray, in conversation they were full of light and fire. His smoothly shaved face revealed a strong square mouth, supported by a broad and prominent chin. Brown denounced slavery in look and language, fierce and bitter. He thought slaveholders had forfeited their right to live and slaves had the right to gain their liberty in any way they could. He did not believe that moral suasion would ever liberate the slave, or that political action would abolish the system. [10]

John Brown confided to Frederick Douglass, he long had a plan to accomplish this end. During his time with Douglass, Brown devoted considerable time to writing a provisional constitution for use after the overthrow of the U.S. government.

On February 4-5, 1858, he sent two letters to his son, John Brown Jr. The elder Brown suggested, "I would like you to make a trip to Bedford, Chambersburg, Gettysburg, and Uniontown, in Pennsylvania, traveling slowly, inquiring with every man on the way, or every family of the right strip, and getting acquainted as much as you can. When you look at the location of those places, you will see the advantage of acquaintances in those parts." [11] Whether his son made an investigative trip to Bedford in 1858 is not known.

Brown traveled through the Northeast raising money for his insurrection during 1858. John Brown traveled back to Kansas and Missouri later that year. He made newspaper headlines again in December 1858. An enslaver was killed in Missouri and 11 enslaved people liberated. Brown evaded authorities while escorting the enslaved people to freedom in Canada. President James Buchanan was under significant pressure to act on the latest incident. Buchanan authorized a reward of $250 for the arrest

Photograph of Frederick Douglass in 1856. (Library of Congress)

of Brown and an accomplice. [12] Brown was now a wanted man and began using the alias names of John Smith, Isaac Smith, and S. Monroe.

John Brown returned to the East Coast in the spring of 1859 to complete plans for the raid on Harpers Ferry. Brown sent a letter on June 23rd from Pittsburgh to John Henrie (Kagi) under the alias S. Monroe. Kagi was John Brown's second in command during the raid at Harpers Ferry. Brown instructed Kagi, "Please inquire for a letter at Bedford, PA. If you do not find one there, you have got ahead of us. Wait a little. If you have any company along, it may be just as well not to appear as fellow travelers. We may begin prospecting before we get to Bedford." The letter confirmed Brown was actively recruiting participants for the raid. [13]

According to a Bedford Gazette article published on 04 November 1859; Brown, two sons, and an accomplice checked into the Bedford Springs on June 25th. Brown and his sons registered under the alias last names of Smith. Later, Benjamin F. Meyers, editor of the Bedford Gazette, claimed he played a game of billiards with Brown above the bowling alley at the back of the hotel. Meyers was introduced to "John Smith" by Colonel Hafer, proprietor of the Springs. Meyers wasn't overly impressed when he met Brown, referring to him as an "elderly gentleman with a taciturn disposition." [14]

Brown met with three black abolitionists, Elias Rouse, John Fidler, and Joseph Crawley. John W. Rouse, son of Elias Rouse, referenced Brown visiting Bedford in a letter written on November 25, 1895. John W. Rouse recalled John Brown being a guest of his father when he was a boy. Their home was at 228 W. Pitt Street. The current house at this address was likely built in a later era. The address of Crawley during the John Brown visit in Bedford County is not known. Brown was actively seeking help for the planned insurrection at Harpers Ferry. Details of the efforts made by Rouse, Crawley, and Fidler are unknown. After Brown's capture, Elias Rouse fled to London, Canada, where he stayed with relatives. He did not return to Bedford until around the beginning of the Civil War. [15] The Gazette article on November 4, 1859 stated, "Reports have circulated some of the colored people in this vicinity, have been connected with the Harpers Ferry affair. We have taken the pains to inquire into the matter and have found no positive evidence, thus far, to implicate them." Brown is believed to have left Bedford on June 27th. President James Buchanan could have almost collected his own reward for the apprehension of Brown. Buchanan checked into the Springs three weeks later for his regular summer holiday at the Bedford resort. [16]

Drawing of the Bedford Springs Hotel by Augustus Kollner in 1840. (Spanierman Gallery, New York)

Some unsubstantiated references to John Brown's stay in Bedford County exist. An anonymous letter to the editor of a local newspaper, on January 27, 1869, claims Brown was very anxious to buy property but was unable to find anything that suited him. Brown allegedly spent a night or two with William Kirk in June 1859. Kirk is listed in the 1860 St. Clair Township Census and was as an active participant in the Underground Railroad. William Kirk lived until 1891 and is buried in the Fishertown Brethren Cemetery. Also referenced was David D. Eshleman of Middle Woodbury Township. Eshleman was allegedly a confidant of Brown, who visited him near Harpers Ferry shortly before the raid. Eshleman is listed in Woodbury Census records. He died in a farming accident in 1864 and is buried in the Germany Valley Cemetery in Shirleysburg. The individual who signed this letter as "H" admitted he didn't have firsthand knowledge of Eshelman traveling to meet with Brown. No other information on the association of Kirk or Eshleman with Brown is known.[17]

John W. Rouse lived in a house at 228 W. Pitt Street in Bedford. The current house shown in this photograph replaced the house Rouse owned.

John Brown requested Frederick Douglass to meet him in Chambersburg in August 1859. A historical marker on route 30 marks the location of a quarry where two titans of the abolitionist movement met. Brown detailed the plans for the Harpers Ferry raid and implored his friend to join him. Brown confided he had a special purpose for Douglass. "When I strike, the bees will begin to swarm, and I shall want you to help hive them." Douglass was adamantly against this action and could not convince Brown to abandon the plan during the next two days. He was convinced Brown was going into a perfect steel-trap and would never get out alive. They parted ways, Douglass returned to Rochester. John Brown proceeded toward his destiny. Frederick Douglass was right. Once surrounded, escape would be impossible.[18]

On October 8th, John Brown wrote a letter to his wife. He provided the names of seven men to contact if assistance was ever needed. Among the seven names written by Brown were Joseph Crowley, Elias Rouse, and John Fiddler of Bedford.[19]

On the sabbath, eight days later, Brown resolutely proclaimed, "men, get your arms, we will proceed to the Ferry." Brown and his small band of 18 followers departed a rented farmhouse a few miles north of Harpers Ferry. They proceeded down a dark, deserted road on a damp, chilly night. John Brown rode in the wagon hauling torches, a sledgehammer, and a crowbar. The insurgents also loaded pikes on the wagon. Pikes were to be issued to enslaved people who were untrained in using firearms. The men marched solemnly in pairs behind the wagon, concealing weapons underneath shawls. Most of the men were in their 20s, five in their group were black, one was an enslaved person. Stated plans for seizing weapons, securing the town, and instigating the uprising were remarkably sparse. There was no fixed hour for withdrawal from Harpers Ferry, no rendezvous location when they left, and no contingency plans if anything went wrong. A blind allegiance to the leader and his lack of tactical and logistical planning would soon prove fatal.[20]

The raiding party crossed a covered bridge over the Potomac River and arrived in the Harpers Ferry business district at 11:00 that night. A gate to the armory was pried open. A dumbfounded watchman was the first of over 60 people taken hostage. Having a flair for the dramatic, Brown sent some of his men to apprehend Col. Lewis Washington, grandnephew of the first president. Lewis Washington lived on a nearby property and was an enslaver. Brown coveted two weapons possessed by the Colonel. A pistol presented to George Washington by Lafayette and a sword gifted by Frederick the Great. Colonel Washington, the weapons, and several enslaved people who were issued pikes, were carted back to the armory.[21]

Around 1:30am, things began to unravel. A train bound for Baltimore arrived in Harpers Ferry. Moments later, an innocent baggage handler was mortally shot. Ironically, the first man to die during the raid was a free black man. The sound of gunfire also alerted many in the town. For some unexplained reason, John Brown allowed the train to proceed several hours later. Brown later lamented not detaining the train was the biggest mistake made during the raid. Telegraph lines around the town had been cut. But once the train arrived at a station with a working telegraph, an urgent message was relayed to authorities in Washington. [22]

Brown expected thousands of enslaved people would quickly join the rebellion. A fundamental flaw in his plan was the lack of a mechanism to inform the enslaved people in nearby areas of the insurrection. Brown's second in command, John Henri Kagi, begged him to leave town throughout the early morning hours. Brown waited too long. By late morning, local militias were arriving and the window to escape had closed. The insurgents were surrounded in a barricaded engine house with their hostages. When asked later why he didn't leave for the Virginia Mountains when he had a chance. Brown provided a characteristic explanation. "It was foreordained to be so. All our actions, even all the follies that led to this disaster, were decreed to happen ages before the world was made." [23]

During the day, four townspeople were killed in gun battles. Several raiders lay dead, including Brown's son Oliver. A second son, Watson, was mortally wounded. Many more on both sides suffered gunshot wounds. President Buchanan tasked Colonel Robert E. Lee, who was at his home in Arlington, with putting down the rebellion. Lee and his aide, Jeb Stewart, rushed to Harpers Ferry, arriving late that evening. They found a drunken, disorganized, and unruly mob of townspeople and militia exchanging sporadic gun fire with insurgents couped up in a small building full of hostages. Lee was relieved to find such a farcical situation. Rumors had been swirling of a larger scale uprising. Lee relayed to Washington; no further troops were needed. Lee posted 90 U.S. Marines based at the D.C. Navy Yard, around the engine house. Because of the danger posed to hostages, he waited until sunrise to end the standoff. [24]

The next morning, only John Brown and six of his men, two of them wounded, remained alive in the crowded engine house. Two other followers were hiding in a nearby building. Jeb Stuart approached the engine house under a flag of truce to request surrender. There were upwards of 2000 spectators peering from every available vantage point in the town. Brown cracked the door open 4 inches with a cocked carbine. Stuart recognized Brown and inquired, "Why, aren't you old Osawatomie Brown of Kansas, whom I once had as my prisoner?" Brown responded, "Yes, but you did not keep me." Stuart previously crossed paths

Harpers Ferry Engine House aka John Brown's Fort on the left from a photograph taken in 1862.
(Library of Congress)

with Brown out west and was the first to confirm his identity at Harpers Ferry. As Lee predicted, Brown refused to give himself up, stating, "No. I prefer to die here." Stuart stepped back and gave the rearranged signal to attack. [25]

A dozen marines used a sledgehammer and a ladder as a battering ram to bust through the doors. The standoff was over in seconds. One marine was dead, along with two more of Brown's insurgents. Brown was stuck several times by a sword but was not fatally injured. Shortly after being freed, Col. Lewis Washington provided the following comments.

> John Brown was the coolest and firmest man I ever saw in defying danger and death. With one son dead by his side, and another shot through, he felt the pulse of his dying son with one hand and held his rifle with the other, and commanded his men with the upmost composure, encouraging them to be firm and to sell their lives as dearly as they could. [26]

There was no middle ground regarding opinions on John Brown. The idea of a white man attempting to spark an armed slave uprising brought outrage and stoked fear in the South. Many in the North admired and sympathized with Brown. The irreconcilable gulf in opinion was expressed in newspapers and in congress. Comments in a Richmond Inquirer, the week after the raid, provide some insights into the Southern frame of mind.

> Harpers Ferry invasion has advanced the cause of disunion, more than any other event that has happened since the formation of the government. There exists a horror and indignation no public meetings can express. It has revived, with tenfold strength, the desire of a Southern Confederacy. [27]

Days after Brown's execution, Jefferson Davis made a declaration from the Senate floor. The attack was grounds for Southerners to leave the Union, "even if it rushes us into a sea of blood." [28]

When news of Harpers Ferry reached the North, reactions of many mirrored the thoughts of abolitionist William Lloyd Garrison. "Though well intentioned, the raid was misguided, wild and apparently insane." Over the next 6 weeks, John Brown's words and demeanor did much to change perceptions, including some not sympathetic to his cause. Brown eloquence before his sentencing was especially moving. The following is an excerpt of his self-defense.

Interior of the Harpers Ferry Engine House, just before the entry gate is breached. Colonel Washington and other hostages are pictured on the left. (Frank Leslie's Illustrated Newspaper - November 5th, 1859)

Now if it is deemed necessary that I should forfeit my life for the furtherance of the ends of justice, and mingle my blood further with the blood of my children and with the blood of millions in this slave country whose rights are disregarded by wicked, cruel and unjust enactments, I say, let it be done. [29]

Authors Walt Whitman and Henry David Thoreau made contributions to Brown's transformation as a martyr. Whitman wrote the poem "Year of Meteors" after witnessing the execution in Charlestown on December 2nd, 1859. Professor Thomas Jackson accompanied cadets from the Virginia Military Institute who were brought in as guards for the execution. A year and a half before gaining the nickname "Stonewall", Jackson was struck by Brown's courage. He commented, "He behaved with unflinching firmness." John Wilkes Booth also witnessed the execution. Booth wrote he was "glad to see the traitor hanged, but the brave old man's bold act had changed history." [30] Standing at the gallows, Brown's last statement befitted a man who looked and spoke like a prophet. "I John Brown am now quite certain that the crimes of this guilty land: will never be purged away; but with Blood. I had as I now think: vainly flattered myself that without very much bloodshed; it might be done." [31]

John Brown remains an enduring symbol of the anti-slavery movement. The insurrection attempt at Harpers Ferry failed miserably, but his holy war on slavery was soon realized. For fire breathing secessionists, the election of Abraham Lincoln months later was the proverbial last straw.

John Brown's last words in his handwriting. (Library of Congress)

Asa Silver Stuckey. (Chandral West)

Chapter 15
Snake Spring Valley, Woodbury, and Bloomfield Township

Three prominent men and their families led efforts to help enslaved people travel safely through Snake Spring Valley, Woodbury, and Bloomfield Townships. The Bedford County bicentennial book, Kernal of Greatness, published in 1971, provided a brief overview of the local Underground Railroad. The following is an excerpt.

> The Underground Railroad played a part in bringing Negroes through and possibly to the county. Complete records were not kept, but the dramatic and daring work of the agents and helpers in the movement is a part of our history.
>
> The fugitives used two routes mainly. One came up through Black Valley and crossed over the Bedford-Chambersburg Turnpike at Mt. Dallas, up the lower Valley Road to Snake Spring, to the Stuckey farm in the valley. Over in Morrison's Cove on this side of Woodbury, the runaways found temporary shelter with the Keagy family. When the timing was right, they moved northward, out of the county. Another branch came up from the Cumberland Valley into Bedford County. [1]

Ben F. Van Horn authored the Bible, Axe and Plow, a history of the Northern Bedford School District area in 1986. Two Underground Railroad stations are cited in the book. The following is the excerpt.

> At least two families in the Cove played prominent roles in helping runaway slaves to flee from Southern plantations to freedom in Canada. Their homes were "stations" on the way north.
>
> Colonel James Madera, the manager of the Bloomfield Furnace, was an ardent abolitionist and provided sanctuary for fugitives on one of the "underground" routes. It is said that his home contained several secret rooms in the cellar at the time. His house is now the modernized residence of Mr. And Mrs. Benjamin Slick, owners of the Bloomfield Furnace Farms north of Bakers Summit.
>
> Another station was the Keagy homestead south of Woodbury. This station was on the "line," as the routes were called, which led from the Maryland border through Black Valley, Mt. Dallas Gap, up the lower Snake Spring Valley Road with a station at the Stuckey farm, over the mountain into Morrisons Cove, through Woodbury, and northward. The Keagy homestead, built in 1813, is now the property and home of Mrs. Paul Ritchey, Sr. [2]
>
> The devious means by which the "conductors" concealed their "passengers" as they moved them to the next station were many. The next station from both the Madera's and Keagy's was on Catfish Ridge, south of Hollidaysburg.

Asa Silver Stuckey was born in Napier Township in 1825. Asa and Sarah Boyd Kinton were married in 1847. They raised six children on a prosperous family farm in Snake Spring Township. The following is an excerpt from a biography of Asa.

> Asa Silver Stuckey is a man of character, ability, and progressive ideas, he became actively identified with affairs of the town and county as one of the leading Republicans of this vi-

Stuckey Farmhouse on Detwiler Lane near Lower Snake Spring Valley Road.

Photograph of Captain John S Stuckey. (Bed. Co. Hist. Society)

cinity. For several years, he served as Justice of the Peace and was a prominent member of the Lutheran church. [3]

By the front door of the house, a removable finial sits on top of a newel post at the bottom of the staircase. Removing the finial exposes a hole that extends to the basement. The hole enabled communications between someone near the front door and freedom seekers hiding in the basement.

Asa's brother, John Silver Stuckey, was a captain in the 138th Pennsylvania Volunteers in the Civil War. John suffered the loss of a leg during the battle of Opequan in 1864. Asa passed in 1889 and Ann in 1910. The Stuckey's are buried in the Mount Olivet Cemetery in Manns Choice. [4]

The Morrisons Cove Herald published an article in 1967 on the Keagy homestead being an Underground Railroad station. Jacob Keagy built a house in 1813 on farm property a half mile south of Woodbury. The article noted the Stuckey farm in Snake Spring Valley and another station in the Catfish Ridge area near Hollidaysburg. [5]

Jacob H. Keagy was born in 1786 in Adams County, Pennsylvania. Jacob married Fanny Longanecker in 1822. They raised 6 children on the family farm. Jacob passed in 1858. Fanny lived to be 95 years old. She was buried beside her husband in the Keagy Cemetery in 1898. The 1850 census listed five Keagy children: David, Catherine, Peter, Ann, and Jacob, living on the Keagy farm. Oldest son, Michael, was living on a separate property in Woodbury with his wife and two small children. The Keagy family worshiped at the Brethren Church in Woodbury. Peter, born in 1834, was a long-time pastor at the church. [6]

The Brethren denomination was an early adopter of anti-slavery doctrine. By unanimous vote at the annual meeting of 1782, the Church of the Brethren stated no member should or could purchase negroes, or keep them as slaves. The annual meeting of 1797 reaffirmed this viewpoint by unanimously voting that no enslaver could be baptized as a member of the church until all slaves were set free. [7]

The Altoona Mirror published an article in 1976 on Colonel James Madara of Bloomfield Township. Madara was a well-known ironmaster who managed the Sarah and Bloomfield furnace operations for Dr. Peter Schoenberger. Madara was also a firm abolitionist. The Madara family lived in a large two-story house with four large rooms on the first floor, six or seven bedrooms on the second, and a partially dug out cellar. Secret spaces in the house used to hide freedom seekers were known only to family members. James Madara was born in Franklin County, Pennsylvania, in 1813 to a family of modest means. James married Jane Wishart in 1833. They were parents of seven children. The following are excerpts from a biography on Madara.

Colonel James Madara started as a day laborer, chopping wood at forty cents a cord. Being

The Jacob H. Keagy house is just south of Woodbury on Route 36.

The James Madera house. Today, the Madera property is the Bloomfield Nursery on Sproul Mountain Road near Roaring Spring. A false wall once existed on the right side of the first floor of the house and the basement below.

Photograph of the basement area in the Madera house where freedom seekers once hid behind a false wall.

James and Jane Madera. (History of Bedford, Somerset and Fulton Counties)

an excellent judge of human nature and possessing all the qualities which command respect and obedience, he could control almost any number of men without an effort. As a furnace man and business manager under Shoenberger, the then king of ironmasters in Pennsylvania, he outranked all others, and enjoyed the greatest respect and confidence of his employer. His success as a businessman was due greatly to promptness in action and determination in purpose. His judgment and dispatch in business matters were unsurpassed, and transactions of small or large amounts were made with astonishing rapidity. During the (Civil) war, he was appointed government iron inspector, with the rank and title of colonel, by Secretary Stanton, which position he filled till the close of the war. As a citizen, no man was more useful or had more influence in his community than he. A leader in all public enterprises, he always endeavored to cast his influence on the side of right and justice. Among his neighbors and business associates, his word was always as good as his bond, because he never allowed either to be protested. His last illness, which was short, was caused by pneumonia, and he died at Bloomfield Furnace, May 2, 1879, grieved for by all who knew him. [8]

The following is an excerpt from Madara's obituary in the Altoona Tribune.

Colonel James Madara was a careful businessman, with a profound judgment and sterling integrity. He was honored and respected at home and abroad. His employees loved him dearly, and many tears will be shed as they remember the charities and deeds of kindness that he sowed as he traveled over the paths of life. He was successful in accumulating considerable of this world's good, but he used them for good purposes. His heart was open to the entreaties and wants of those whom he could befriend. He was friendly to churches and supported Sunday schools. No man in this community will be so much regretted as he will be His place will be hard to fill, for "None knew him but to love him, none named him but to praise." [9]

No stories survive on specific Underground Railroad efforts of the Stuckey, Keagy, or Madara families. Freedom seekers were often routed toward Hollidaysburg from the Keagy and Madara houses. One incident was published in the Altoona Tribune in 1913. The following is an excerpt from the article.

David Brown, the aged colored resident of Hollidaysburg, was intensely interesting because he talked about local happenings incident to the famous "Underground Railroad" to Canada. "When a runaway slave from the south got into Hollidaysburg," he said, "the southern slave owners never got them back." One time in 1858, when I was about 12 years old, the colored people of Hollidaysburg found four slaves hiding on Chimney Rocks. They brought the fugitives down and put them in the jail for safekeeping. Major Hewit was district attorney. He didn't want to send the slaves back, so he left town when the hearing was to come off, and a young lawyer, Essington Hammond, took his place, The Hon. S.S. Blair defended the slaves at the hearing, which went against the slaves. Mr. Blair told the authorities who were trying to take the slaves back, that they'd have to get them past the Hollidaysburg colored people first. They found out Mr. Blair was right. The next morning, the colored people got together and, together with some of the white citizens, took the slaves from the jail and hid them among our homes. Then they were sent on northward to Canada. [10]

An obituary of a former enslaved person published in the Altoona Tribune on March 26th, 1916, also referenced Chimney Rocks. The obituary mentioned David Brown helped William Jackson and his father when they fled slavery. This is possibly the same David Brown cited in the previous 1913 article. The following are excerpts of the William Jackson obituary.

> William Jackson, one of the oldest and best known colored residents of Hollidaysburg, died on Friday morning at 7:15 o'clock at the Blair County hospital of fatty degeneration of the heart and other diseases incident to old age. He had been able to work up until a few months ago, but recently his health failed rapidly and two weeks ago he was removed to the hospital. He was born at Mercersburg, VA and was aged at death about 75 years, when a young man he and his father, who were slaves in Virginia, ran away from their master's plantation and made their way northward a short time prior to the breaking out of the Civil war. One day in their travels, the father and son arrived at Hollidaysburg by way of Cumberland and Bedford. They paused on the Chimney Rocks ridge to rest and were found there by David Brown, of Hickory Street, who was taking a stroll with his dog, the animal discovering the fugitives and leading his master to them. They told Mr. Brown that they had run away from their master and asked him to shield them. He went back to his home near the foot of the ridge and told his father and brothers, who guided by Dave, went back to the ridge, and brought the men home with them. They stayed at the Brown home for a few days when they secured employment on the farm of Judge Smith at Mentzer's Mills. The deceased worked there for a number of years, later coming to Hollidaysburg, where he has resided ever since, his father preceding him to the grave some years ago. He was a member of the A. M. E. Zion church of Hollidaysburg for many years and was possessed of a kindly and generous nature that made him many warm friends. [11]

Chimney Rocks was a predominantly black section of Hollidaysburg and a center of Underground Railroad activity. Chimney Rocks is located on the right side of route 36 when approaching the town from the south. Catfish Ridge is also mentioned in Underground Railroad stories. Chimney Rocks sits on Catfish Ridge which runs south of Hollidaysburg along route 36.

Possibly the best-known Underground Railroad operator in Blair County was William Nesbit. William

Photograph taken from Chimney Rocks Park on Catfish Ridge. The town of Hollidaysburg is shown in the distance.

was born in Carlisle in 1822 and moved to Hollidaysburg in 1841. He married the following year and became a well-known barber in Blair County. The following is an excerpt from his obituary in 1895.

> Mr. Nesbit was a man who labored all his life for the elevation and the good of his race. During the prevalence of slavery, he was always an active worker in the schemes of the "underground railway," and many a negro is living today who first tasted of freedom through the efforts of Mr. Nesbit and his associates. He was connected with the Union League and was a prime mover and one time president of the State Equal Rights League. This society had for its object the securing for the colored people the rights accorded them under the fifteenth amendment to the constitution of the United States. In 1880, he was a delegate to the Republican state convention, held in Harrisburg. He was also largely instrumental in securing for his people the right to enter public conveyances, such as steam and other railway cars, on equal footing with the whites. In fact, his entire life was devoted to the elevation of the colored race, and to this end he toiled unselfishly, scorning means that were base and employing only the weapons he could best use - a fearless heart, a shrewd and courageous mind, and an untiring hand. [12]

William Nesbit's barbershop was located in Hollidaysburg on the corner of Montgomery and Allegheny Street in the Exchange Hotel. William and his wife, Sarah Thomas Nesbit, lived on 409 Walnut Street. They moved to Altoona in 1855 to a residence on the corner of 10th and 16th Street. William and Sarah are buried in the Hollidaysburg Union Cemetery. Their son, William W. Nesbit, was a corporal in the 54th Massachusetts, the most famous Black regiment of the Civil War. The 1989 movie, "Glory", is the story of the 54th Massachusetts and their heroic actions during the second battle of Fort Wagner. [13]

Among the noted Underground Railroad conductors in Blair County were two other black barbers, Daniel Hale Williams, Jr and Sidney Carr. The son of Daniel Hale Williams, Jr. was a world-famous doctor. Daniel Hale Williams III performed the first successful heart surgery in 1893. He also founded the Provident Hospital in Chicago, the first black owned hospital in the United States. [14]

Sidney Carr may be connected to the well-known story of a freedom seeker being rescued from slave catchers in Hollidaysburg in 1855. The Jacob Green story is covered in chapter 12 - Cumberland Valley. A version of the story from another source noted a Snyder Carr, a black barber, grabbed Jacob Green's arm and dragged him from the grasp of a slave catcher. Carr and several other individuals whisked Green to Chimney Ridge south of Hollidaysburg. From there, Jacob Green continued his journey to Canada. [15]

Reverend James Graham of the A.M.E. Zion church in Hollidaysburg was a known supporter of the Underground Railroad. John Fidler, Joseph Crawley, and Elias Rouse were black leaders of the Underground Railroad in Bedford. Fidler was a preacher in the A.M.E. Zion church, Crawley was a barber, and Rouse worked in both vocations during his lifetime. The leaders of both the Bedford and Hollidaysburg Underground Railroad, being preachers and barbers, are not coincidences. Churches were the center of community life and barbershops were social gathering places. Both afforded ample opportunities for communications beneficial to Underground Railroad operations.

Others in the surrounding areas were associated with the Underground Railroad. Morris Walker, son of Benjamin H. Walker of Pleasantville, cited the names of three Blair County agents named Low, Showmo, and Cypher. Thomas Henry, a circuit rider in the A.M.E. Zion church, provided invaluable support to enslaved people seeking freedom. The Thomas Henry story is reviewed in chapter 9 - Cumberland Maryland. Some known area safe houses north and west of Hollidaysburg were operated by William Slick in Geistown, Abraham Andrews Barker in Ebensburg, and Samuel and Jean Lemon in Gallitzin. The Lemon House Tavern has been recognized as a National Underground Railroad Network of Freedom site by the National Park Service. [16] Many enslaved people also hid in churches and in the homes of unknown numbers of free blacks during their journey north.

Chapter 15 - Snake Spring Valley, Woodbury, and Bloomfield Township

Photographs of Daniel Hale Williams and the hospital he founded. (Williams family tree on Ancestry.com)

Daniel Hale Williams historical marker. (HMdb.org)

Abraham Andrews Barker - Underground Railroad agent in Ebensburg (John Griffith)

The Lemon House Tavern in Gallitzin. (National Park Service)

Mark Miller and wife Mary Calhoun Miller. (Larry Peterson)

Hiram Way circa 1875. (Ancestry.com)

Photograph of the Samuel Way House in 1971. (Bedford County Historical Society)

Photograph of the "Mount Miserable Hill" cited in the Mark Miller story. The location is near the Indian Eve Road and Pine Grove Church Road intersection. The Miller farm was between this location and Route 56.

Chapter 16
Fishertown and Pleasantville
The Quakers

No church denomination is more closely associated with the anti-slavery movement than the Quakers. The Quakers were early adopters of viewpoints highlighting the evils of slavery. In 1688, Quakers in Germantown, Pennsylvania issued a proclamation on the immorality of slavery. In 1774, the church adopted a resolution stipulating any Quaker involved with slavery must give up all associations with this sin or leave the denomination. A noted abolitionist played a key role in the church splitting into Orthodox and Hicksite branches in 1828. Influential leader Elias Hicks placed more emphasis on the Quaker tenet of "Inner Light" than traditional Orthodox preachers. Hicksite followers were more inclined to support radical actions against slavery. [1] Many Hicksite Quakers near Fishertown and Pleasantville helped runaways pass through the county.

One of the first Quaker stations north of Bedford was the Eli Miller farm near the intersection of Route 56 and Indian Eve Road. Thomas Miller and Hiram Way are mentioned in the following story. They are the sons of well-known Underground Railroad agents, Eli Miller and Samuel Way. The Samuel Way farm is a neighboring property, a short distance north of the Miller property on Route 56. The following is a verbatim transcript of information provided by Mark Miller, Eli Miller's youngest son. Mark Miller was born in 1839.

> At the time referred to in this sketch, Eli Miller lived upon what is now known as the Claycomb farm, on Dunning's Creek, in East St. Clair township, on the road leading from Fishertown to Osterburg. On a Sunday evening in about the year 1840, Thomas Miller, then a lad about twelve years old, was watering horses at the creek when he discovered four colored men sitting on the foot-log which crossed the creek near the watering place. They made inquiry as to their whereabouts, when Thomas told them to remain where they were until he had sent his father down to see them. Mr. Miller then went down, and after a short interview took them in charge, gave them something to eat, and furnished them appropriate shelter for the night. The next morning, fearing that their captors might come upon them before he could arrange for their removal to a more advanced station, he secluded them in a dense wood or thicket back of "Mount Miserable Hill," an abrupt elevation above the present county bridge. This was a rather secure fortress, as their position was accessible from the main road only on foot, and the elevation of such as to afford them a good view of surroundings. Here they were kept for three or four days and nights, when, by the assistance of John Albaugh, they were transferred under cover to Benjamin Walker's, who took them afoot across the mountain, Benjamin riding a white horse along the road, and the darkeys taking to the woods for safety, being guided in their course by keeping an open eye on the white horse. On landing at William Sleek's they were soon forwarded to Johnstown, and probably got into the friendly hands of Mr. Cover, Mr. Helsop, or Avery Allen. We should have noted in passing, that, in fifteen minutes after leaving Miller's, the pursuers of these poor fellows passed by the place from which they had so recently started, and two boys, Thomas Miller and Hiram Way, being in a shed by the roadside, heard them discussing the subject of capturing these slaves. [2]

Isaiah P. Blackburn provided additional information on the efforts of his grandfather, Eli Miller. The following are some excerpts from a letter sent to Wilbur H. Siebert.

My grandfather, after bringing two men down from the hill under cover of darkness, hid them in the left of a pigpen that stood by the roadside. In a little while, two men rode up and stopped only a few feet away from their quarry. One of them voiced the belief that was where the "damned old Quaker" lived. The other one thought not, and so they rode on. Good old Granddad lost no time in getting started in the other direction with his passengers.

The other most active ones in such work in this immediate neighborhood were Nathan Hammond, who lived on Hammond Hill a half mile to the northeast, William Kirk nearby, Samuel Way and John Albaugh and two of my grand uncles Samuel and Josiah Penrose, who lived in Quaker Valley one mile to the north.

At Pleasantville, 5 miles to the north (Alum Bank) Benjamin Walker, George Harbaugh, Samuel, George, and John Hess took over. It was their business to deliver "customers" across the Allegheny Mountains to the home of William Sleek (heretofore mentioned) in Geistown, from which point they were advanced into Clearfield County. But on occasion they would be taken from this section to Hollidaysburg by way of Claysburg and East Freedom for these men followed one of Nature's physical laws–the line of least resistance–and when the mountain roads were full of slave hunters, they chose the safer way. [3]

Photograph of Samuel Kirk Miller, younger brother of Eli Miller. Samuel is cited as an Underground Railroad agent in the History of Bedford and Somerset Counties book. No stories about his activities have survived. (Meri Waterhouse)

Underground Railroad agent William Kirk is referenced in the Blackburn letter. Kirk was a community leader and Civil War veteran. William Kirk was mentioned as possibly meeting with John Brown during his stay in Bedford County prior to the Harpers Ferry Raid. The following is a William Kirk biography published in the History of Bedford, Somerset, and Fulton Counties in 1884.

William Kirk came from York County to Fishertown in 1839, learned the potter's trade and worked at it for several years in Fishertown and in other parts of the state. He was in partnership with Jacob Fisher in the manufacture of pottery from 1852 until 1855, when the pottery was burned. Mr. Kirk then purchased twenty-seven acres of land and erected a new pottery, which he still continues to run. He served in the army in the 149th Regt. Penn. Vols. from February until May 1865. Mr. Kirk was jury commissioner for five years and mercantile appraiser two years. In 1862 he was United States deputy marshal of St. Clair township. In 1870, he took the census of several townships and boroughs. He has served as school director and in 1883 was elected justice of the peace. [4]

Photograph of Sarah Blackburn Kirk, wife of William Kirk. (Ancestry.com)

Isaiah P. Blackburn also provided some information on his other grandfather, James Blackburn. James Blackburn's 1837 diary entry detailed the story of the two runaways, Patrick and Abraham. The first of several violent confrontations in this story took place in Bloody Run (Everett) and is retold in chapter 11 - Bloody Run & Rainsburg. The following are excerpts of two stories on the Underground Railroad activities of James Blackburn.

Sometimes even a Quaker was driven to subterfuge or evasion. Grandfather James Blackburn was taking a load of "grain" over the mountain, though as a matter of fact it was a number of sacks stuffed with chaff under which two slaves were hidden. He was stopped on the way by two hunters who inquired if he had seen any Negroes along the road. He answered soberly and truthfully that he hadn't seen a colored man since he left home, though he knew that the boys they wanted were only five feet away.

On another occasion, he had made a safe delivery to (Mr.) Sleek and on his return trip, he met up with hunters. He engaged them in a friendly conversation for a long a time as possible and then shrewdly steered them into a mountain road which he knew right well didn't lead into Geistown at all. [5]

The following biography of James Blackburn was published in the History of Bedford, Somerset, and Fulton Counties in 1884.

James Blackburn was born in Menallen Township, Adams County, Pennsylvania, February 22, 1797. In 1803, he was removed to live with his uncle, Benjamin Bowen, just east of where the village of Pleasantville now stands. Of his immediate family, there were two sisters and four brothers. Being left orphans, they were scattered during their childhood, but finally all settled in the same neighborhood, married, and raised large families, averaging nine children each. In the year 1820, James married Anne Penrose, daughter of Amos and Sophia Penrose. They had thirteen children. For many years, he was the principal man in his neighborhood, who was called upon to write articles of agreement, deeds, wills, and very often letters, for those who could not write them for themselves. He often taught school during the winter season, frequently settled up estates, and was a practical surveyor. A nephew who has since been a county surveyor was a student of his. When the free-school system in Pennsylvania went into operation under the law of 1834, he was appointed a member of the first board of school directors and assisted in dividing the township into school districts and building schoolhouses. He subsequently served several terms as school director, and also as assessor, at different times. In the Society of Friends, of which he was a lifelong member, he was often called upon to serve as clerk, both in the monthly and quarterly meetings, and he was an elder at the time of his death, which occurred in 1869. [6]

The Blackburn biography referenced Amos Penrose. Amos is the grandfather of Joseph Penrose. Joseph responded to a request from I. H. Betz for information on the Underground Railroad. The Penrose family farm was located north of Fishertown near the Friends Cemetery in Spring Meadow. The following is a verbatim transcription of a January 29th, 1904, letter written by Penrose.

Friend Hiram Blackburn handed me your letter of Jan. 26th, directed to him in which you would like information in regard to the Underground Railroad, which was so gloriously carried on in Bedford County during the days of slavery in the country. Well Mr. Betz, I am 58 years old, born of descendants of Friends or Quakers, of which it is useless to say was always found to be anti-slavery people. But now to the point that you ask for. This railroad ran from Cumberland, Maryland to Altoona, Pa., and on through Center County and further than that I am not able to give you any account and can only speak of the line from Bedford North—but this one colored man Rev. Fidler I was well acquainted with, and a fine colored man he was-From Bedford this line run North, and on that line Friends (or Quakers) in the following order—Samuel Way, David Way and then to Samuel Way and Cyrus Way and then came Amos Penrose and William and Thomas Penrose (brothers of Amos) and Amos Penrose two sons, Josiah and Samuel Penrose, of which I am a son of the latter-and our own farm, where my Grandfather lived when this work was being carried on. I could show you the hiding place today, where in a lonely place in the rocks on my grandfather's farm, where when I was but a small boy, I first saw the first runaway slaves. My grandfather Amos Penrose always seen to us giving them their meals and at this time he had three to feed-two big colored men and a woman. When we went to their hiding place, this colored woman grabbed me and kissed me and then commenced to cry as though her heart would break and said that she had a little boy that she left at home, just my size. This was my first experience, and I shall never forget it, and suppose it happened when I was about three years old (1849). It was about ten miles north of Bedford and was the first station after leaving Bedford and called the Quaker Settlement. Then Northwest

Joseph Penrose. (Undated newspaper obituary photo)

Joseph Penrose and his wife Hester Lucretia Mock Penrose, pictured in the middle of the photograph, lived well into the 20th century. Joseph passed in 1930 at age 84. Hester Lucretia passed in 1948 at age 93. (Carole Carlson)

Photograph of Amos Penrose Family Farm in 1904. A story has been retold of a hidden trapdoor on the first floor of the farmhouse, which opened to a small unexcavated area of the basement. (Carole Carlson)

of this was a family by the name of Walker that came to the County from Adams County. The old gentlemen's name was Abner, and he had a son Benjamin Walker that done a great deal on this line. I have heard my grandfather Samuel Penrose and Uncle Josiah say that there never was a slave caught by their owners after it passed into Benjamin Walker's hands. Of course there was plenty of men in those days that lived along the line that was in sympathy with the work and a good work it was, but when the genuine work had to be done the Ways, Penroses and the Walkers had to do it—As have said from this North to Center County, cannot give any names for as you will see by my age I was young and the line was destroyed by the hand and pon of the greatest man that was ever born in this or any other country-Abraham Lincoln. If this proves to be an account to you, you are welcome to it-if not-just throw it into the waste basket. -Yours Respectfully- Joseph Penrose. [7]

Joseph Penrose was among the many devout Quakers in Bedford County who were Civil War veterans. Quakers are well-known for pacifist convictions. Church doctrine was firmly against both slavery and violence. Quakers considering enlisting in the war, faced an agonizing decision on conflicting beliefs of their faith. Those who chose to fight resolved the conundrum by choosing the lesser of evils. [8] As a small boy, Joseph was deeply affected by the experience of seeing an enslaved mother weeping about a child being left behind. Joseph enlisted in the war twice. He first volunteered in the 21st Pennsylvania Cavalry and reenlisted with the 205th Pennsylvania Infantry.

Joseph was close to another Quaker soldier, first cousin and neighbor Benjamin H. Garretson. The Garretson farm was the first property south of the Friends Cemetery in Spring Meadow. The Penrose farm was next to the Garretson property. Both farms were on the west side of route 56. Joseph was 18 and Benjamin was 21 when they volunteered in the 21st PA Calvary in July 1863, days after the battle of Gettysburg. Both reenlisted in the 205th PA Infantry in August 1864. They served side by side in the same company during the siege of Petersburg. [9]

Joseph and Benjamin took part in a horrific charge on the Fort Mahone earthworks at Petersburg on April 2nd, 1865. During a months-long siege, Union soldiers referred to Fort Mahone as Fort Damnation. During the early morning assault, artillery poured double cannister shot on Union soldiers charging toward Confederate lines. Cannister shot was a fearsome shotgun type munitions fired out of a cannon. While being fired on, soldier in the 205th tore through wooden obstacles, plunged into a rain filled ditch, and scaled Confederate earthworks. Once they reached Confederate trenches, desperate hand to hand combat took place with bayonets and rifle butts. [10] During the charge, Benjamin Garretson suffered a severe head wound and was rushed to a hospital in Philadelphia for treatment. No record exists of Joseph Penrose being wounded during the April 2nd assault.

Benjamin's older brother, Josiah P. Garretson, enlisted in the 55th Pennsylvania infantry in February 1864. The 55th PA also took part on the April 2nd assault. On that day, Josiah and Benjamin were in different parts of the sprawling Petersburg battlefield. Josiah did not find out his younger brother was gravely wounded until receiving a letter from their mother on April 19th. Josiah rushed to his brother's side at the hospital. Benjamin succumbed to his wounds on May 27th, 1865. The next day, Josiah went to Philadelphia to arrange for an undertaker to embalm his brother's body. Benjamin Garretson is buried at the Friends Cemetery at Spring Meadow. He was 23 years old when he died. Robert E. Lee's Confederate Army surrendered at Appomattox on April 9th, 1865. Both Josiah Garretson and Joseph Penrose returned home in June 1865. [11]

  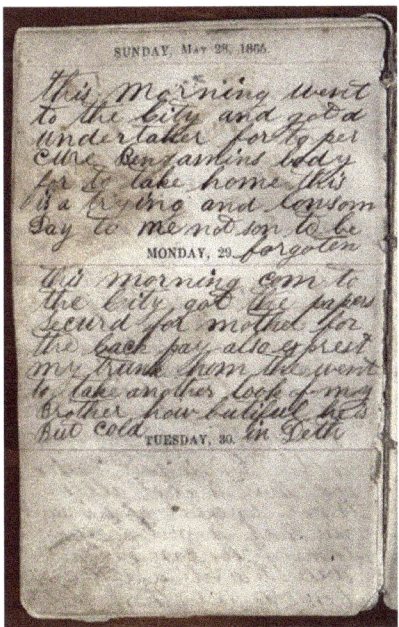

(left) Josiah Garretson. (center) Benjamin Garretson. (right) Photograph of Josiah Garretson's diary. Josiah wrote in the Sunday, May 28th entry, "This morning went to the city and got an undertaker for to percure Benjamin's body to take home. This is a trying and lonesome day to me, not soon to be forgotten." (Charles Garretson)

Many other Quakers living near Fishertown and Pleasantville fought in the war. Some farewells before leaving home, ended up being last goodbyes between loved ones. John Allison, Joseph Blackburn, Levi Blackburn, Benjamin H. Garretson, William H. Miller, and William A. Walker lost their lives during the war and are buried in the small Friends Cemetery in Spring Meadow. Emanuel Harbaugh is buried in the Mount Union Cemetery in Lovely. Martin Blackburn is buried at the Andersonville POW camp cemetery. Eli Harbaugh, George W. Harbaugh, and Wilson Harbaugh are buried in national cemeteries in southern states. The final resting places of John Harbaugh and Robert Harbaugh are unknown. Many on this partial listing of Quaker soldiers who perished during the war are family members of Underground Railroad agents.

Around 70 Bedford County soldiers in the 91st Pennsylvania infantry enlisted a month prior to the battle of Boydton Plank Road near Petersburg in October 1864. Nine county soldiers suffered casualties during the battle, including three who lost their lives. Thomas G. Walker was one of the soldiers who took part in this battle. [12] Thomas is the son of a well-known Underground Railroad conductor, Benjamin H. Walker of Pleasantville. After the war, Thomas retold a story of four freedom seekers from Alabama. The North Star guided the runaways prior to making contact with supporters of the Underground Railroad. The following is a transcript of the story.

Photograph of Isaac and Mary Minerva (Harbaugh) Walker, and daughter Midge Sybil (Walker) Mock circa 1895. Isaac was enlisted in the 205th PA and took part in the tragic early morning assault on April 2nd with Benjamin Garretson and Joseph Penrose. (William Roy Mock)

> In 1848 or '49 four negroes from the state of Alabama. arrived along the underground railroad at a point in the mountain below Bedford Springs. It was a rare occurrence that fugitives from such a great distance succeeded in making their way to the north. Soon after they started from their master, they found themselves pursued by bloodhounds, a mother dog, and three pups. One of the negroes knew the old dog very well, and, calling her to him, he stuffed the bell which she had on her neck with moss, so as to prevent its ringing, and the pups, being unable to follow their mother, became scattered and returned home; besides this, the negroes, on crossing a stream, followed down the same some distance before coming out on the other side, so as to defeat further pursuit of hounds. From their mountain retreat, they pressed on toward Pleasantville, evading the main road and guided by the north star. On arriving at Benjamin Walker's they were conducted by him to the top of the mountain, and were there directed to William Sleek's, as many others had previously been. Their would-be captors were in close pursuit, as they were met by Mr. Walker on his return down the mountain. As their capture was not heard of afterward, it is to be presumed that they finally escaped into Canada. [13]

Portrait of Thomas G. Walker. Thomas was enlisted in the 171st PA and 81st PA Infantry during the Civil War. (Ronn Palm)

Three other sons of Benjamin H. Walker enlisted in the same Union Army regiment. Asahel, Benjamin and Morris Walker volunteered in the 84th Pennsylvania infantry. Several other local Quakers also volunteered in this regiment including Thomas Garretson, Jason Harbaugh, William H. Harbaugh, and William H. Miller. The 84th PA infantry took part in heavy combat during the battles of 1st Kernstown, Chancellorsville and the Wilderness. Morris Walker later detailed a story of a freedom seeker that took place in November 1848. The following is a verbatim transcript of a story of a runaway retracing his steps to avoid capture.

> On the day of General Taylor's election as President of the United States, or possibly the day following, a giant negro slave came to Walker's by some route unknown to the informant and remained there several days. At one time during his stay, he was secluded in the haymow, concealing himself underneath the hay. Some children playing in the barn at the time were jumping from the upper logs of the building down upon the hay, and repeatedly landed upon the spot underneath which he was located. This sport was much less entertaining to him than to the children, and he was finally obliged to reveal his hiding place, much to the surprise of the youngsters, as can be readily imagined. On looking out of the gable of the barn he spied his master passing nearby on an old bald-faced horse which had long been a great favorite of his on the old plantation, and it required the exercise of all his courage to keep from calling out and giving himself up to his owner. Suppressing this feeling, however, he kept in seclusion for a day or so, and then, in order to evade capture by pursuing that course, he was brought back under cover of darkness by Josiah Penrose and Eli Miller to the Quaker Settlement, whence he was afterward taken on another route to Hollidaysburg. Here were parties, also, by the name of Low, Showmo and Cypher, who were friends to such fugitives, and who doubtless advanced him to Center County for still further guidance. [14]

Five sons of Benjamin Walker joined the Union Army: Asahel, Benjamin H., Isaac, Morris, and Thomas G. All five brothers were able to return home. In 2006, a Pennsylvania Historical and Museum Commission historical marker was erected close to the Benjamin Walker homestead near Pleasantville, recognizing efforts in the Underground Railroad.

George Harbaugh was also honored on the Walker Homestead roadside marker. The Harbaugh family experienced much tragedy during the Civil War. Two sons of George Harbaugh enlisted in the Union Army. Wilson Harbaugh died of disease within a month of enlisting in the 55th Pennsylvania Infantry in 1864. Joseph Harbaugh enlisted in the 79th Pennsylvania Infantry and survived the war. Ten nephews of George Harbaugh joined the Union Army.

Photograph of Josiah Edwards. Josiah enlisted in the 55th PA Infantry in March 1864 and was discharged on a Surgeons Certificate in March 1865. The photo shows Josiah posing with a crutch. No casualty records were found on his injury. Charles Blockson noted Josiah's father, Amos Edwards, in a book published in 1981 on the Underground Railroad in Pennsylvania. (Gari Jensen)

Jason Harbaugh. Nephew of George Harbaugh. Jason returned home in 1864 after experiencing heavy combat in the 84th PA Infantry. (Bedford Co. Hist. Soc.)

Four never returned home. The four who perished were enlisted in the 55th Pennsylvania Infantry. Eli Harbaugh died of smallpox in 1862, John Harbaugh died of disease in 1863, Both George W. Harbaugh and Robert Harbaugh died of wounds suffered during the initial assault of Petersburg in 1864. [15]

The following is a Benjamin H. Walker obituary published in the Altoona Tribune in 1896.

> One of the most important "engineers" on the underground railway, Benjamin H. Walker, died on Thursday at his home in Alum Bank, aged 81. He was born 1808. in York County, this state, and in 1827 moved, from thence in company with his father's family, to Bedford County. The year following, he and his father walked to Ohio and back in search of a more desirable location for a home, but eventually settled in what is now West St. Clair township, Bedford County. Benjamin H. Walker was the father of eleven children, having raised of this number, six sons who served honorably in the late war. As early as 1848, he was actively engaged with the system of assistance to escaping slaves known as the underground railway, in that year alone having helped to freedom twenty-seven fugitives. At that time the route led from Virginia through Maryland via Cumberland valley, in Bedford County, to Bedford. The station here was in charge of Joseph Crawley, John Fiddler and Elias Rouse, all of whom have died. From Bedford, the route led to Alum Bank or Pleasantville, as it was then known.
>
> On the premises of Mr. Walker beneath a shed had been prepared a compartment where slaves were fed and rested until an opportunity arose for moving them on ward. Not an unusual method of transportation from this point was the loading of slaves into a large wagon, cover them with hay, and the wagon frequently mounted by the veteran kind-hearted, sympathetic Quaker "engineer," hauled to Johnstown or Altoona. At the latter place, the late William Nesbit, a lifelong friend of Mr. Walker, took the slaves in charge.
>
> No adequate means for learning the exact number of "passengers" nor the "underground system" is in our possession, but certain it is learned from contemporaries of those whose time and every effort were devoted to the cause, that the escaping slaves who were met, entertained, and forwarded guardedly to the next "depot" by Mr. Walker would amount up in the hundreds. [16]

The following is a biography of Walker published in the History of Bedford, Somerset, and Fulton Counties in 1884.

> Benjamin H. Walker, of Pleasantville, came from York county to St. Clair township in 1827, and has since followed farming and shoemaking. He was postmaster of Alum Bank from 1869 to 1882. Mr. Walker was a strong anti-slavery man in the days when the word abolitionist was a term of reproach. Preceding the war, he was an indefatigable worker on behalf of the slaves and one of the leading operators of

Nancy (Minnie) Edwards Harbaugh, wife of George Harbaugh. (Jonathan Caruana)

Abner Walker. (William Roy Mock)

Benjamin H. Walker. (William Roy Mock)

the underground railway. He has assisted fully five hundred fugitives to gain their liberty, often keeping several of them concealed about his premises for weeks together. When he considered the opportunity favorable, he would fill bags with straw, load his sleigh or wagon with them, and, concealing the negroes beneath the bags, take the load across the mountains, as if going to market. He delivered the fugitives into the hands of other friends, who assisted them further on their way toward freedom. For many years a standing reward of five hundred dollars was offered for the apprehension of Mr. Walker, and his life was often in danger. [17]

The 1904 letter written by Joseph Penrose to I. H. Betz contained the following recollection, "I have heard my grandfather Samuel Penrose and Uncle Josiah say that there never was a slave caught by their owners after it passed into Benjamin Walker's hands. The History of Bedford and Somerset Counties book included a story of two enslaved runaways being captured in Alum Bank (Pleasantville) prior to reaching the Walker homestead. The following is the transcription.

The Benjamin Walker Homestead historical marker is near Pleasantville at the Rainbow Drive and Beutman Road intersection.

It was a short time prior to the Civil war when two slaves found their way into the so-called Quaker settlement, with the evident hope of procuring assistance in their journey northward. Somewhere in the vicinity named they met two men by name of Mock and Crissman, who, it seems, knew of a reward being offered for the capture of a certain two slaves, and who, under the pretense of being friendly to their interests, induced the negroes to be locked up in an old school-house nearby, while arrangements would be made for their conveyance to some northward station. The captors at once went to Bedford and got into communication with their master, who promptly came on, identified his property, paid the prize money to the captors and returned home with his possession of human souls. This was one of the few instances, if not the only one, of like character which occurred in the neighborhood of the underground railway people of this section.

To the sore disappointment of the poor slaves, we can well imagine, there would be added the oppression and vengeance of a tyrannical master when back on the old plantation. On the other hand, to the treachery and deception of the captors, there was added the contempt and reproach of every good citizen of the community in which they lived. Neither of them prospered after this event. Mr. Mock soon afterward came to an untimely death by being shot at Alum Bank while attempting to escape from the custody of a squad of soldiers who had been de-

Photograph of Benjamin H. Walker's wagon bench resting on the "Old Conemaugh Path." This path is also referred to as the "Old Johnstown Road" and the "Old Bedford Pike." The wagon bench is on display at the Dunnings Creek Friends Museum in Fishertown. (William Roy Mock)

Photograph of the old schoolhouse cited in Mock and Crissman slave catchers story. (History of Bedford and Somerset Counties book)

Photograph of a small stone foundation on a hill about a half mile east of Pleasantville on Route 96. Confirmation could not be made on this being the foundation of the schoolhouse cited in the story.

tailed to preserve order at an election in St. Clair township, and who had him under arrest for disturbing the peace. Numerous afflictions and misfortunes followed Mr. Crissman during the several years which he lived afterward, and whilst he, no doubt, ofttimes regretted his conduct and would have undone the deed if such were possible, he never regained the confidence or respect of the people.

The school-house in which the slaves were imprisoned or detained is located on the road leading from Osterburg to Alum Bank, and about a half mile distant from the latter place. We refer now to the original Alum Bank, or Rinniger's farm, not Pleasantville, where the post office is of that name. The building is now owned by Henry Geible and is occupied by a tenant as a residence. [18]

The first name of the individual referred to as Mr. Crissman is unknown. Crissman was a common name in this era in St. Clair Township. Frederick Mock and the story of Mock being killed on an election day in 1864 is well known. The following is a transcript of an article, Murder in St. Clair, published in the Bedford Gazette on October 14th, 1864.

> On Tuesday evening last, a young man named Trout, of St. Clair township, accompanied by three armed soldiers, followed Mr. Frederick Mock, of that township, when on his way home from the election, and overtaking him, seized him and marched him several miles, when Mr. Mock endeavored to make his escape. The soldiers immediately fired upon him and killed him. Mr. Mock was not a conscript, had not resisted the draft in any form, but was a peaceable and useful citizen. He was deliberately murdered in cold blood, merely because he was an active Democrat. We denounce this foul and bloody deed, as an outrage not to be tolerated by any people. We call upon the military, as well as the civil authorities, to have the perpetrators of this cowardly murder brought speedily to justice, and we warn them that if they fail to do it, there is a sleeping lion that will be roused from his lair, before whose roar the very earth shall tremble. The blood of Frederick Mock cries from the ground for vengeance against the men at whose instigation soldiers were placed at the polls on Tuesday last. Let them beware! [19]

The Bedford Inquirer did not cover the incident the week Mock was killed. As with most controversies, the Gazette and the Inquirer offered vastly differing perspectives. The following are excerpts of a lengthy Inquirer article published on February 24th, 1865, the week James Trout was acquitted of the murder. The "unscrupulous partisan sheet" cited in this article is a reference to the Bedford Gazette.

> It appears about the time the polls closed, a number of persons grossly and repeatedly insulted Gideon D. Trout, the father of the defendant. That this was done by pre-concert, and with design to induce a fight. That after long forbearance, Mr. Trout, roused by fresh insults to passion beyond control, rushed upon one of his traducers. and a fight ensued, in which he was knocked down and terribly beaten. That during this fight, Frederick C. Mock struck James Trout across the face with a rifle gun, with such force he was knocked back three or four steps, fell to the earth, and the bones of his nose fractured.
>
> During the melee, it appears, two of the soldiers interfered to keep the peace, and that Frederick C. Mock, who was armed with revolver and rifle, drew his rifle upon one of them. The sergeant thereupon ordered three of his men to go after and arrest Mock. The soldiers arrested him, he attempted to escape, and received his death wound, at the hands of the soldiers, by a musket ball. The violent death of Frederick C. Mock is exceedingly to be regretted. It never would have occurred but for the crowd of ruffians and black-guards who lingered around the place of election after the polls had closed and insulted Gideon.
>
> We do not justify the soldiers in what they did. They were sent into a neighborhood notoriously disloyal, on the difficult and dangerous duty of arresting deserters and conscripts who had failed to report. Looking at the remote causes, Frederick C. Mock owes his death to the perverted sentiment of a part of the Democracy of Bedford County, who have been educated by an unscrupulous partisan sheet, and by unscrupulous partisan leaders, into a belief that the war is unjust and wrong; that the draft is unconstitutional and illegal, and ought to be resisted. [20]

Isaiah P. Blackburn also noted the animosity existing in the area during the Civil War era. The following is an excerpt from a letter sent to Wilbur H. Siebert, who requested information on the Underground Railroad.

> My grandfather (James Blackburn) lived four miles west of here (Fishertown) at what was then "Six Roads" now Ryot, among the foothills of the Alleghenies. That section was then infested with Southern sympathizers and slave baiters, known as "Copperheads." So he operated under something of a handicap, but he did it just the same. During the war, his barn was burned because of his loyalty. [21]

Another story of enslaved people being captured in St. Clair Township appeared in the Bedford Inquirer on October 10th, 1856. A falsehood was being circulated on the eve of an election. A county candidate for Associate Judge was rumored to have been a slave catcher. The article clarified several runaways were caught the previous year in St. Clair Township, but the slave catcher's name was Samuel Barnhart, not Adam Barnhart, who was running for Associate Judge. The article noted the two men were not remotely related. [22] A Samuel Barnhart died in 1863 and is buried in the Bedford Cemetery. No other information was found on an individual with this name.

Many Underground Railroad agents in Cambria County helped freedom seekers after they were ushered over the mountain from Bedford County. The known agents include William Slick, Sr. of Geistown; Dick Bacon, William Barnett, Pade Carns, John Cushon, Wallace Fortune, Mr. and Mrs. James Heslop, Frederick Kaylor, William "Mose" McLain, John Myers, Isaac Weatherington, and Henry Willis of Johnstown, and Abraham A. Barker of Ebensburg. Eli Miller's son, Mark Miller, also cited a Mr. Cover, a Mr. Helsop and Avery Allen as agents in Johnstown. [23] Many enslaved people hid in homes of an unknown number of free blacks during their journey North.

Thomas G. Wright operated a station at a nursery south of Pleasantville. Decades after the movement ended, his granddaughter wrote a letter referencing the Underground Railroad. Mary Wright Eaton noted her grandfather and Benjamin Walker were conductors on the railroad. She cited childhood memories of meeting a "very elderly looking, tall Negro with snow white hair" in the 1880s. The man was sitting on the porch at the Walker homestead, visiting with Benjamin. She was told the man was an enslaved person who had been helped across the mountain by the railroad. [24]

Recommended reading for anyone interested in the Bedford County Underground Railroad is "The Last Station: Underground Railroad of Quaker Corner" by William Roy Mock. The book provides detailed historical information on the anti-slavery views of the Quaker Church and the efforts of the local Quaker community in Fishertown and Pleasantville to help enslaved people. The names of several other Underground Railroad agents are referenced in this book, including Rebecca Walker, Samuel A. Sleek, Amos Edwards, George Hess, Samuel Hess, and William Wright. Copies of the book are available at the Bedford County Historical Society.

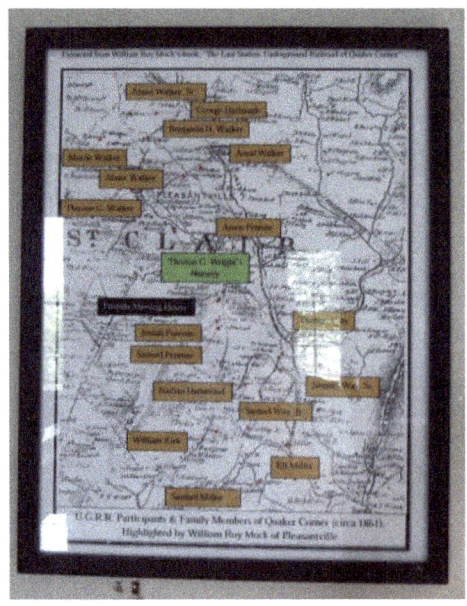

Photograph of a property location map of the Fishertown and Pleasantville Underground Railroad agents. Displayed at the Dunnings Creek Friends Museum in Fishertown. (William Roy Mock)

Chapter 17
Conclusion

Other structures have been rumored as possible Underground Railroad stations in Bedford County. No documentation was found connecting Underground Railroad activities to any buildings not listed in this book. Folklore often surrounds taverns, inns, and hotels that predate the Civil War. Local slave catchers were known for frequenting taverns, and slave catchers from the south sought overnight accommodations. Therefore, these types of public places would not have been ideal locations for Underground Railroad stations. People fleeing slavery were much more likely to have hidden in private residences.

Research for the book revealed some interesting findings. On the eve of the Civil War, the 1860 census recorded over 250,000 free blacks living in southern slave states and Washington, D.C., including around 170,000 free blacks who resided in Virginia, Maryland, Delaware, and D.C. Fewer free blacks lived in northern states, around 220,000. [1]

Some enslaved people gained freedom because of evangelical church movements that influenced enslavers to end the practice of slavery. Harriette Bradley cited the Great Revival movements in southern evangelical churches at the turn of the 19th century were a factor in recently freed people coming to Bedford County. Her research paper noted, "Many slaves were set free when whites had to give up the practice of owning these unfortunates or give up church membership." [2] Anti-slavery church doctrine may have also influenced the transition of some county families from enslavers to Underground Railroad supporters. Limited information was found on the personal motivations of this transition. Contents of the heart may not be easily quantifiable.

A cloak of secrecy surrounded the Underground Railroad while it operated. Few participants wrote of their support of the movement after it ended. There are several possibilities why efforts were rarely documented. The Civil War was a traumatic time for many in Bedford County. Families who did not suffer the loss of loved ones certainly would have known others not as fortunate. Many soldiers returned home maimed or traumatized from witnessing horrors. After the war, some supporters likely moved on with their lives, putting all issues surrounding the Civil War behind them. Underground Railroad agents may have also been reluctant to write about breaking federal laws, regardless of strong convictions on the righteousness of the cause. Another factor was the harsh political environment prior to and during the Civil War. The highly inflammatory vitriol printed in Bedford County newspapers provides insight into the divisiveness of the era. Supporters of the Underground Railroad would have been aware of others who were against the war and indifferent to slavery in southern states. Many supporters likely had little interest in revisiting such a divisive time.

Researching the Underground Railroad is analogous to working on a jigsaw puzzle and realizing some of the pieces are missing. A debt of gratitude is owed past generations for providing enough pieces of this puzzle to enable a partial picture to emerge. This partial picture contains many shades of gray. Some clues offer more questions than answers. Those who could answer questions have long since passed. But unanswered questions should not discourage the study of this subject.

Some aspects of the Underground Railroad are unquestioned. Limited numbers of stories survive, but countless more compelling narratives have been lost to history. Other topics will continue to be debated. We will never know the number of runaways that crossed the Bedford County border. Estimates vary widely on the total number of enslaved people who fled into northern states. What we know is northern support of enslaved runaways infuriated the south and helped to hurl the country toward a war that ended slavery in America. The sun set on the Underground Railroad movement only after over 600 Bedford County men and boys perished in a terrible Civil War. If slavery had not existed in America, many of the highly contentious issues that divided the north and south would also not have existed. The controversies and consequences of the antebellum era remain with us today.

Acknowledgements

Local historians provided important pieces of the Bedford County Underground Railroad puzzle. A special thank you is extended to the following people who contributed to this book:

William F. Fine for reviewing the contents and suggesting improvements,

Barbara Sponsler Miller & Carolyn Carroll (Bloody Run),

Patricia Morgart & Jerry Cessna (Rainsburg),

Regina Williams (Chaneysville),

Debra Topinka (Cumberland Valley Township),

William Roy Mock (Fishertown & Pleasantville),

Harriett L. Gaston & Jim Snyder, Jr. (Blair County),

Barbara Zaborowski (Cambria County),

Bedford County Historical Society: Gillian Leach, Linda Norris, Pat Harrison, Pam Morgart, Thierry Drenning, Janet Bowser, and Bob Way (Bedford County).

Notes

Chapter 1 - Introduction

1. Pinsker. "Vigilance in Pennsylvania: Underground Railroad," *PHMC*, 2000, p.42, 90, https://gis.penndot.gov/CRGISAttachments/Survey/2000-H001-042.pdf.

2. "Chesapeake & Ohio Canal." *National Park Service*, 15 December 2020, https://www.nps.gov/choh/learn/historyculture/thecanalarrivesincumberland.htm

Longfellow. Rickie. "The National Road." *U.S. Department of Transportation*, 30 June 2023, https://www.fhwa.dot.gov/infrastructure/back0103.cfm

3. Switala. *Underground Railroad in Pennsylvania*, 2008, p.29

4. Siebert. *The Underground Railroad from Slavery to Freedom,* 1898, p.7.

5. Siebert. *The Underground Railroad from Slavery to Freedom,* 1898, p.48.

6. Webster, Ian. "CPI Inflation Calculator," *Official Data Foundation,* https://www.officialdata.org/us/inflation/1850?amount=1000.

7. "Death of Rev. John Fidler – A Veteran Gone to Rest." *Everett Press*, 2 October 1891, p.3.

8. *History of Bedford, Somerset and Fulton Counties,* Waterman, 1884, p.293.

Chapter 2 - Overview

1. Siebert. *The Underground Railroad from Slavery to Freedom,* 1898, p.59.

2. Hall, William M. *Reminiscences and sketches*, p. 58-61.

3. Siebert. *The Underground Railroad from Slavery to Freedom,* 1898, p.59-62.

Wilson. *History of the rise and fall of slave power*, 1872, p.65.

4. Gara. *The Liberty Line: the Legend of the Underground Railroad*, 1961, p.46-48.

5. "A Slave Stampede." *Herald of Freedom and Torch Light*, Hagerstown MD, 5 May 1857.

Wilson. *History of the rise and fall of slave power*, 1872, p.78.

6. Siebert. *The Underground Railroad from Slavery to Freedom,* 1898, p. 56-57.

"The Underground Railroad. *Emmanuel Parish of the Episcopal Church*, accessed 17 May 2023, https://www.emmanuelparishofmd.org/emmanuel-and-the-underground-railroad/.

7. Pinsker. "Vigilance in Pennsylvania: Underground Railroad," *PHMC*, p.31.

"Vigilant Committee and the Underground Railroad." *Historical Society of Pennsylvania*, accessed 7 November 2023,https://hsp.org/sites/default/files/legacy_files/migrated/vigilancecommitteeofphiladelphia_master.pdf and https://www.portal.hsp.org/unit-plan-items/unit-plan-51.

8. Siebert. *The Underground Railroad from Slavery to Freedom,* 1898, p.87.

Wilson. *History of the rise and fall of slave power*, p.65.

Origins – Chapter 3

1. "What was New Netherland." *New York State Library,* 1 November 2022, https://www.nysl.nysed.gov/

newnetherland/what.htm.

Siebert. *The Underground Railroad from Slavery to Freedom*, 1898, p. 19.

2. Siebert. *The Underground Railroad from Slavery to Freedom*, 1898, p. 45.

3. Pinsker. "Vigilance in Pennsylvania: Underground Railroad," *PHMC*, p. 14,

4. Siebert, *The Underground Railroad from Slavery to Freedom*, 1898 p. 33.

5. Armistead. *Life of Anthony Benezet*, Sherman & Company Printers, Philadelphia, 1859, p.15.

6. "Benjamin Rush Portal on Abolition and Race." *University of Pennsylvania*, accessed 23 March 2023, https://guides.library.upenn.edu/benjamin-rush/Rush_on_Abolition_and_Race.

7. "Frederick Town Herald, 11 June 1803. p.3." *The Maryland State Archives, Legacy of Slavery in America*, accessed 18 November 2023, http://slavery2.msa.maryland.gov/pages/Search.aspx.

8. Siebert. *The Underground Railroad from Slavery to Freedom*, 1898, p. 34.

9. Wilson. *History of the rise and fall of the slave power in America*, 1872-77, p.63.

10. Siebert. *The Underground Railroad from Slavery to Freedom*, 1898, p. 28.

11. "100 Dollars Reward." *Frederick Town Herald,* 14 April 1819, p.3.

12. *The Kernal of Greatness*, Bedford County Heritage Commission, 1971, p.73.

13. Van Horn. *Bible, Axe and Plow*, 1986, p.125.

14. Siebert. *The Underground Railroad from Slavery to Freedom*, 1898, p. 43-44.

15. "Fifty Dollars Reward." *Maryland Advocate*, 4 June 1833, p.1.

16. "Index to Hagerstown Papers – The Herald of Freedom and Torch Light, 18 March 1847." *Washington County Library*, p. xii, https://www.washcolibrary.org/assets/documents/NewsIndex_Slavery1845-1854.pdf.

17. Siebert. *The Underground Railroad from Slavery to Freedom*, 1898, p. 44.

18. Schell, William P. "In Olden Time! Reminiscence of Days Agone," *Bedford Gazette*, 22 Jun 1906, p.1.

19. "Local Items." *Altoona Tribune*, 17 April 1862. p.3.

Fugitive Slave Legislation – Chapter 4

1."Pennsylvania - An Act for the Gradual Abolition of Slavery, 1780." *The Avalon Project: Documents in Law, History and Diplomacy,* accessed 16 March 2023, https://avalon.law.yale.edu/18th_century/pennst01.asp.

2. Cannon, Alexandria. "Gradual Abolition Act of 1780," *George Washington's Mount Vernon,* https://www.mountvernon.org/library/digitalhistory/digital-encyclopedia/article/gradual-abolition-act-of-1780/.

 "An Act for the Gradual Abolition of Slavery (1780)." *UShistory.org,* Accessed 3 November 2023, https://www.ushistory.org/presidentshouse/history/gradual.php.

3. Young, Cory James. *"For Life or Otherwise: Abolition and Slavery in South Central Pennsylvania, 1780-1847."* Phd. dissertation – Georgetown University, 17 June 2021, p.11-13, https://repository.library.georgetown.edu/bitstream/handle/10822/1062658/Young_georgetown_0076D_15039.pdf.

4. "Indentured Servitude." *Merriam-Webster Dictionary*, accessed 3 November 2023, https://www.merriam-webster.com/dictionary/indentured%20servant.

"Indentured Servitude." *Wikipedia,* accessed 3 November 2023, https://en.wikipedia.org/wiki/Indentured_servitude.

5. Siebert, *The Underground Railroad from Slavery to Freedom*, 1898, p.21-22.

6. "Pennsylvania Personal Liberty Law (1826)." *Dickinson College,* accessed 4/11/23, https://blogs.dickinson.edu/hist-288pinsker/pennsylvania-personal-liberty-law-1826/.

7. Mosvick, Nicholas. "Prigg v. Pennsylvania," *National Constitution Center*, accessed 4/11/23, https://constitutioncenter.org/blog/on-this-day-the-supreme-court-decides-prigg-v-pennsylvania.

8. "Index to Hagerstown Papers – The Herald of Freedom and Torch Light, 18 March 1847." *Washington County Library*, p. xiii, https://www.washcolibrary.org/assets/documents/NewsIndex_Slavery1845-1854.pdf.

9. Pinsker. "Vigilance in Pennsylvania: Underground Railroad," *PHMC*, 2000, p.45-46,

10. "A Scrap of Local History." *The Altoona Tribune*, 12 Apr 1883, p.3.

11. "Dred Scott v. Sandford (1857)." *National Archives*, accessed 4/14/23, https://www.archives.gov/milestone-documents/dred-scott-v-sandford.

12. VanderVelde. *Mrs. Dred Scott: A Life on Slavery's Frontier,* 2009, p.3.

White, Helen McCann. "The Lawrence Taliaferro Papers," *Minnesota Historical Society*, 1966, p.5-11. http://www2.mnhs.org/library/findaids/m0035.pdf.

"Missouri's Dred Scott Case 1846-1857." *Missouri State Archives,* accessed 6 November 2023, https://www.sos.mo.gov/archives/resources/africanamerican/scott/scott.asp.

Coen, Rena N. "Eliza Dillon Taliaferro: Portrait of a Frontier Wife." *Minnesota History 52, no. 4 (Winter 1990)*, p.146-153.

13. Greenberg. *Dred Scott and the Dangers of a Political Court*, Lexington Books, 2010 p.26.

VanderVelde.*Mrs. Dred Scott: A Life on Slavery's Frontier,* 2009, p.233.

14. *History of Bedford, Somerset and Fulton Counties*, Waterman, 1884, p.207.

"Missouri's Dred Scott Case 1846-1857." *Missouri State Archives,* accessed 6 November 2023, https://www.sos.mo.gov/archives/resources/africanamerican/scott/scott.asp.

Murdoch family tree information. *Ancestry.com.*

15. Nilsson, Jeff. "Mr. Lincoln Discusses His Proclamation," *The Saturday Evening Post*, 22 September 2012, https://www.saturdayeveningpost.com/2012/09/emancipation-proclamation/.

16. Pinsker. "Vigilance in Pennsylvania: Underground Railroad," *PHMC*, p. 52-53.

Early Black History in Bedford County – Chapter 5

1. Smith, Larry. "Slave & Indentured Servant Records," *Genealogical & Historical Research in Old-Bedford County*, http://www.motherbedford.com/GenBook91.htm, 2000.

2. Schell, William P. "In Olden Time! Reminiscence of Days Agon," *Bedford Gazette,* 22 Jun 1906, p.1, https://www.newspapers.com/image/15482147/?terms=%22William%20P.%20Schell%22&match=1.

Bradley, Harriette. "Negroes in Bedford County" *Bedford County Historical Society*, 1976.

The Kernal of Greatness, Bedford County Heritage Commission, 1971, p.72.

3. Bradley, Harriette. "Negroes in Bedford County," *Bedford County Historical Society*, 1976.

4. Pinsker. "Vigilance in Pennsylvania: Underground Railroad," *PHMC*, p.22.

5. Schell, William P. "In Olden Time! Reminiscence of Days Agone," *Bedford Gazette*, 22 Jun 1906, p.1.

6. "Colored Citizen Share in Bedford Traditions." *Bedford Gazette*, 25 Mar 1948, p23.

Preston Stewart page, *Findagrave.com,* https://www.findagrave.com/memorial/114875479/preston-stewart.

7. *The Kernal of Greatness,* Bedford County Heritage Commission, 1971, p.73

Bradley, Harriette. "Negroes in Bedford County," *Bedford County Historical Society*, 1976.

8. *The Kernal of Greatness*, Bedford County Heritage Commission, 1971, p.74.

9. Hood J.W. *One hundred years of the A.M.E. Zion Church,* 1895, p.174-177.

10. Documentation provided by Paul Crawford Sr., founder of the Cumberland Valley Township Historical Society, Information courtesy of Debra Topinka.

11. "Colored Citizen Share in Bedford Traditions." *Bedford Gazette*, 25 Mar 1948, p23.

Bradley, Harriette. "Negroes in Bedford County," *Bedford County Historical Society*, 1976.

12. Karns. *Historical sketches of Morrisons Cove*, Altoona Mirror Press, 1933, p.25

History of Bedford, Somerset and Fulton Counties, Waterman, 1884, p.304.

13. "Colored Citizen Share in Bedford Traditions." *Bedford Gazette*, 25 Mar 1948, p23.

Henry Barks family tree, *Ancestry.com*.

14. "Well-Known Negro Policeman is Dead." *The Pittsburgh Post,* 27 December 1906, p.2.

15. "Colored Citizen Share in Bedford Traditions." *Bedford Gazette*, 25 Mar 1948, p23.

16. Schell, William P. "In Olden Time! Reminiscence of Days Agone," *Bedford Gazette*, 22 Jun 1906, p.1.

"Colored Citizen Share in Bedford Traditions." *Bedford Gazette*, 25 Mar 1948, p23.

17. Schell, William P. "In Olden Time! Reminiscence of Days Agone," *Bedford Gazette*, 22 Jun 1906, p.1.

18. George Washington Williams family tree, *Ancestry.com.*

Berlin, Ira. "Soldier, Scholar, Statesman, Trickster" (review of John Hope Franklin's biography of George Washington Williams), *The New York Times*. Retrieved 33 March 2023. https://archive.nytimes.com/www.nytimes.com/books/99/08/15/specials/franklin-williams.html.

19. Mearkle, Kevin. *Civil War Soldiers of Bedford County*, p.335-336.

20. Bradley, Harriette. "Negroes in Bedford County," *Bedford County Historical Society*, 1976.

21. "Colored Citizen Share in Bedford Traditions." Bedford Gazette, 25 Mar 1948, p23.

22. Bradley, Harriette. "Negroes in Bedford County," *Bedford County Historical Society*, 1976.

23. "Colored Citizen Share in Bedford Traditions." *Bedford Gazette*, 25 Mar 1948, p23.

24. Schell, William P. "In Olden Time! Reminiscence of Days Agone," *Bedford Gazette*, 22 Jun 1906, p.1.

"House Speaker Biographies." *Pennsylvania House of Representatives,* https://www.legis.state.pa.us/cfdocs/legis/SpeakerBios/SpeakerBio.cfm?id=62.

A Divisive Time – Chapter 6

1. *The Kernal of Greatness*. 1971, p.76-77.

2. Hall, William M. *Reminiscences and sketches,* 1890, p. 60.

3. "In our paper of the 19th December.*" The Bedford Inquirer and Chronicle ,* 2 January 1857, p.2 (The Bedford Inquirer and Bedford Chronicle merged in 1854. Chronicle was dropped for the name of the newspaper in November 1857.)

4. "Old Abe's War." *Bedford Gazette*, 26 April 1861, p. 1.

5. "House Divided Speech." *National Park Service*, accessed 22 May 2023, https://www.nps.gov/liho/learn/historyculture/housedivided.htm.

6. "For the Bedford Gazette." *Bedford Gazette*, 24 May 1861, p2.

7. "Who Are The Real Traitors." *Bedford Gazette*, 16 August 1861, p.1.

8. "Presidential Election – 1860." *Bedford Gazette,* 16 November 1861, p.2.

9. *Pennsylvania 1860 Census Records*, https://www2.census.gov/library/publications/decennial/1860/population/1860a-30.pdf.

The official Union Army age range for enlistments was 18 to 35 until 1863, when it increased to 45. The 1860 Bedford County Census listed 3330 white males between the ages of 20 and 39. Census records didn't break out the 18 to 19 and 40 to 45 age groups separately.

Mearkle, Kevin. *Civil War Soldiers of Bedford County*, 2021.

10. "Gump letter to the Gazette." *Bedford Gazette*, 24 May 1861, p.2.

"In Memoriam." *Bedford Gazette,* 25 November 1864, p.2.

11. "The Election of 1864."*American Battlefield Trust*, referenced Hallowed Ground Magazine article, Fall 2014, https://www.battlefields.org/learn/articles/election-1864.

"Official Vote of Bedford County for President." *Bedford Inquirer,* 18 November 1864, p.3.

"Satterfield letter to the Inquirer." *Bedford Inquirer*, 18 November 1864, p.3.

12. Braun, Kathryn, "Divided Loyalties: Benjamin and Willian Franklin," *Monticello*, 21 March 2021, https://www.monticello.org/research-education/blog/divided-loyalties-benjamin-and-william-franklin/.

"U.S. Participation in the Great War." *Library of Congress*, https://www.loc.gov/classroom-materials/united-states-history-primary-source-timeline/progressive-era-to-new-era-1900-1929/united-states-participation-in-world-war-i/.

Geography and Transportation – Chapter 7

1. *United States Census Report*, https://www.census.gov/library/publications/1864/dec/1860a.html.

2. "Chesapeake & Ohio Canal – The canal arrives in Cumberland." *National Park Service,* 15 December 2020 .https://www.nps.gov/choh/learn/historyculture/thecanalarrivesincumberland.htm.

Longfellow, Richie. "The National Road." *U.S. Department of Transportation,* 30 June 2023, https://www.fhwa.dot.gov/infrastructure/back0103.cfm.

3. "The National Road." *National Park Service*, June 2009, https://www.nps.gov/fone/learn/historyculture/upload/FONE%20National%20Rd%20SiteB_NBl_pc_columns-head.pdf.

4. Jordan. *The National Road,* 1948, p. 224-227.

5. Searight. *The Old Pike, a History of the National Road*, 1894, p. 109.

6. "James Harris – Accomplice to slave flight, p.2." *Maryland State Archives*, https://msa.maryland.gov/megafile/msa/speccol/sc5400/sc5496/003300/003394/html/003394bio.html.

7. "The Underground Railroad at Mt. Clare." *The B&O Railroad Museum*, https://www.borail.org/collection/the-underground-railroad-at-mt-clare/.

"A Desperate Leap of Liberty." *National Park Service*, https://www.nps.gov/articles/-a-desperate-leap-for-liberty-the-escape-of-william-and-ellen-craft.htm.

8. "Chesapeake & Ohio Canal – The canal arrives in Cumberland." *National Park Service,* https://www.nps.gov/choh/learn/historyculture/thecanalarrivesincumberland.htm.

9. Snyder, Timothy R. "The Chesapeake & Ohio Canal and the Underground Railroad, Along the Towpath," *Western Maryland's Historical Library,* accessed 19 November 2023, http://www.whilbr.org/CandOCanal/Chesapeake-and-Ohio-Canal-the-Underground-Railroad.

"Reverend Hillhouse Buel – Accomplice to slave flight." *Archives of Maryland*, 11 September 2003, https://msa.maryland.gov/megafile/msa/speccol/sc5400/sc5496/010500/010599/html/010599bio.html.

10. "Notes from Nearby article." *Shepherdstown Register*, 04 October 1900, https://www.newspapers.com/image/466381133/?clipping_id=128097422&fcfToken=eyJhbGciOiJIUzI1NiIsInR5cCI6IkpXVCJ9.eyJmcmVlLXZpZXctaWQiOjQ2NjM4MTEzMywiaWF0IjoxNjg5MTg3NTU1LCJleHAiOjE2ODkyNzM5NTV9.RGfERj-NOKx4kgOugVaNK03cCj-uh2RWxuR92tBLg_Y.

11. Switala. *Underground Railroad in Pennsylvania*, 2008, p.29

12. Wallace. *Indian Paths of Pennsylvania,* PHMC, 1965, P. 181-184.

13. Pinsker. "Vigilance in Pennsylvania: Underground Railroad," *PHMC*, p.91.

North Star – Chapter 8

1. "Frederick Douglass Newspapers, 1847 to 1874." *Library of Congress*, https://www.loc.gov/collections/frederick-douglass-newspapers/about-this-collection/.

2. "North Star to Freedom." *National Park Service,* accessed 4/17/23, https://www.nps.gov/articles/drinkinggourd.htm.

3. "Follow the Drinking Gourd. " *Follow the Drinking Gourd: A Cultural History*, accessed 4/17/23, http://www.followthedrinkinggourd.org/.

4. Siebert, The Underground Railroad, 1898, p.54.

5. Drew. *A North-side View of Slavery*, 1856. p.105-109.

6. Pinsker. "Vigilance in Pennsylvania: Underground Railroad," *PHMC*, p.32.

7. Snowberger, Ella M. *Recollections of By-Gone Days in the Cove-Volume 7,* Morrisons Cove Herald, 1939, p.59.

Cumberland Maryland – Chapter 9

1. McMinn, Teresa. "Local ties to the Underground Railroad," *Cumberland Times-News*, 28 December 2019, https://www.times-news.com/news/local_news/local-ties-to-the-underground-railroad/article_306332f6-1844-11ea-a95a-5b8a96ead82e.html.

2. "The Underground Railroad Story." *Emmanuel Parish of the Episcopal Church*, https://www.emmanuelparishofmd.org/.

"Reverend Hilhouse Buel biography." *Archives of Maryland*, 11 September 2003, https://msa.maryland.gov/megafile/msa/speccol/sc5400/sc5496/010500/010599/html/010599bio.html.

3. Henry, Thomas W. *Autobiography of Rev. Thomas W. Henry of the A.M.E. Church,* Baltimore, 1872, p.6-10, https://docsouth.unc.edu/neh/henry/henry.html.

4. Henry, Thomas W. Autobiography, p.56.

Thomas W. Henry family tree, *Ancestry.com.*

5. "Circuit riders spread spirituality via horseback." *Main Line Times & Suburban*, 23 September 2021, https://www.mainlinemedianews.com/2010/06/22/ml-history-circuit-riders-spread-spirituality-via-horseback/.

6. Henry, Thomas W. *Autobiography*, p.19.

7. Henry, Thomas W. *Autobiography*, p.45.

8. Henry, Thomas W. *Autobiography*, p.48-50.

9. "A word to our Southern Neighbors." *Bedford Gazette,* 25 April, 1961, p.2.

10. "Allegany County, MD, and Bedford County, Penn'a. To the Citizens of Pennsylvania." *Bedford Inquirer,* 10 May 1861, p.2.

11. "Camp at Bedford," *Bedford Inquirer*, 10 May 1861, p.2.

Chaneysville – Chapter 10

1. Map of Bedford County, PA, Surveyed, Drawn & Published by G.L. Walker, 1861.

2. Searight. *The Old Pike, A history of the National Road*, p. 263

3. Information on the hotel tunnel provided by Don C. Carns, Sr.

Piper family photographs and information family tree. *Ancestry.com.*

"The National Road." *National Park Service*, June 2009, https://www.nps.gov/fone/learn/historyculture/upload/FONE%20National%20Rd%20SiteB_NB1_pc_columns-head.pdf.

4. Architectural Survey File. *Maryland Historical Trust,*

Ancestry.com family tree information.

5. Jordan, Bill. "View from the Terrace," *Bedford Gazette*, 29 May 1964.

6. *The Kernal of Greatness*, 1971, p.73.

7. Dom, Harriet Griffin. Imes Family Historical Paper, 1978, courtesy of Regina Williams.

8. "Know Your County Tours - Southampton Township." *Pioneer Historical Society*, 1988.

9. Baughman, Jon. "Fugitive Slaves begged to be killed, instead of returning to the Plantation." *Bedford Gazette and Broad Top Bulletin – four-part series*, June & July 2012.

10. Dickey, Gary Alan. *Spurgeon Family History,* 1993.

11. Siebert. *The Underground Railroad from Slavery to Freedom*, 1898, p. 59.

12. Drew. *A North-side View of Slavery*, 1856, p.52.

13. Ellisor, John T. "Creek War of 1813 and 1814," *The Tennessee Historical Society,* 1 March 2018, https://tennesseeencyclopedia.net/entries/creek-war-of-1813-and-1814/.

Bloody Run and Rainsburg – Chapter 11

1. "Five Names." *Bloody Run Historical Society*, https://bloodyrunhistory.org/fivenamesx.html.

2. "The Underground Railroad." *History of Bedford and Somerset Counties*, 1906, p.379-381.

"Underground Railroad in Johnstown." *Sandyvale Memorial Gardens & Conservancy,* http://www.sandyvalememorialgardens.org/heritage/underground-railroad/.

3. 1840 St. Clair Township census records.

Family tree information. *Ancestry.com.*

4. Griffith, Randy. "Area was hub for Underground Railroad," *The Johnstown Tribune-Democrat*, 28 February 2010.

1840 Richland Township census.

5. Hall. *Reminiscences and sketches,* 1890, p. 60.

6. Bradley, Harriette. "Negroes in Bedford County," Bedford County Historical Society, 1976.

7. Juneteenth Underground Railroad Celebration – Downtown Bedford, *2010 program*.

8. Records of the County Governments (Microfilm Copies); Series Title: R47-Bedford County Slave Records, *Pennsylvania Historical and Museum Commission;* Harrisburg, PA.

9. Barndollar family tree. *Ancestry.com.*

History of Bedford, Somerset and Fulton Counties, Waterman, 1884, p.313-315.

10. Barndollar family history information provided by Barbara Sponsler Miller and Carolyn Carroll.

11. Barndollar family tree. *Ancestry.com.*

"William Barndollar obituary." *Everett Press*, 27 April 1906, p.1.

1850 Colerain Township census records

12. 1840-1880 West Providence Township census records.

13. Berlin. *Generations of captivity: a history of African-American slaves*, 2003, p.272.

Cannon, Alexandria. *Gradual Abolition Act of 1780,* accessed 20 November 2023, https://www.mountvernon.org/library/digitalhistory/digital-encyclopedia/article/gradual-abolition-act-of-1780/.

14. Barndollar family tree. *Ancestry.com.*

15. Mearkle, Kevin. *Civil War Soldiers of Bedford County Pennsylvania*, 2021, p. 372.

16. Snowberger, Ella, M. *Recollections of Bygone Days in the Cove – Volume 8*, Morrisons Cove Herald, 1940, p. 75-77.

17. Barth, Louis F. "*Methodism in Everett 1809-1975,"* History Pamphlet on the Everett Methodist Church, 1975.

18. Wesley. "*Thoughts upon Slavery,"* 1778.

19. Siebert. The Underground Railroad from Slavery to Freedom, 1898. p. 94.

20. Bradley, Harriette. "Negroes in Bedford County," *Bedford County Historical Society*, 1976.

Cumberland Valley – Chapter 12

1. Bedford County Press, *Black history of Bedford County,* 12 March 1976, p3.

Bradley, Harriette. "Negroes in Bedford County," *Bedford County Historical Society*, 1976.

John Cessna Morgart family tree family. *Ancestry.com.*

2. 1830 Colerain Township Census.

John Cessna Morgart family tree family. *Ancestry.com.*

3. Hall. *Reminiscences and sketches,* 1890, p.59-60.

4. Ancestry family information on the John Morgart family.

5. "Route from Cumberland, Md., to Bedford PA." *Courtesy of the Ohio History Connection,* Wilbur H. Siebert Collection, 23 December 1895.

6. Wyatt Perry family tree. *Ancestry.com.*

7. Bradley, Harriette. "Negroes in Bedford County," *Bedford County Historical Society*, 1976.

The Kernal of Greatness, 1971, p.73-74.

8. "Death of Rev. John Fidler – A Veteran Gone to Rest." *Everett Press*, 2 October 1891, p.3.

9. "A Reminiscence of Interest to the Older Citizens of the County." *Altoona Tribune,* 12 April 1883, p.3.

10. "The 1858 Kidnapping of Richard Newman." *Blairsville Area Underground Railroad*, accessed 20 November 2023, https://undergroundrailroadblairsvillepa.com/new-page-2.

11. MacCabe. *Parsons' family history and record*, 1913, p. 255-256.

12. Pennsylvania Death Certificate, Corilla Perry – died 18 January 1930 in Johnstown PA. *Ancestry.com.*

Stump and Parsons family trees. *Ancestry.com.*

Stump and Parsons family pages. *Findagrave.com.*

13. "Colored Citizen Share in Bedford Traditions." Bedford Gazette, 25 Mar 1948, p.23.

Henry Barks family tree, *Ancestry.com.*

14. "Well-Known Negro Policeman is Dead." *The Pittsburgh Post,* 27 December 1906, p.2.

15. "Colored Citizen Share in Bedford Traditions." Bedford Gazette, 25 Mar 1948, p.23.

16. "Kidnapping." *Bedford Inquirer,* 2 November 1860, p. 2.

17. "Kidnapper Caught." *Bedford Inquirer"* 9 November 1860, p. 2

18. Gilchrist, Annie M. "Kidnapping in Bedford," *Bedford Inquirer*, 19 September & 26 September 1950.

Mearkle, Kevin. *Civil War Soldiers of Bedford County,* detailed Alphabetical listing.

19. Pinsker. Vigilance in Pennsylvania: Underground Railroad, *PHMC*, p.61.

20. "Two men from Bedford County PA." *Hagerstown Torch Light*, 6 Nov 1835.

21. "Two men from Bedford County." *The Adams Sentinel*, 16 Nov 1835, p.2.

22. *History of Bedford, Somerset and Fulton Counties*, Waterman, 1884, p.220-224.

"Death of Thomas R. Gettys." *Bedford Inquirer*, 30 Mar 1860, p.2.

Thomas R. Gettys family tree. *Ancestry.com.*

23. Conrad Rohm family tree. *Ancestry.com.*

24. "Home Matters." *Pittsburgh Weekly Gazette*, 14 Jun 1851, p.3.

25. "A negro has been tarred and feathered." *The Liberator*, 29 Aug 1856, p.3, http://fair-use.org/the-liberator/1856/08/29/the-liberator-26-35.pdf.

Pinsker. Vigilance in Pennsylvania: Underground Railroad, *PHMC*, p. 91.

26. "Route from Bedford County into Southwestern Cambria County." *Courtesy of the Ohio History Connection*, Wilbur H. Siebert Collection, 5 December 1944.

27. Gara. *The Liberty Line:the Legend of the Underground Railroad,* University of Kentucky Press, 1961, p. 55.

Bedford – Chapter 13

1. "John M. Rouse letter to Wilbur Siebert." *Courtesy of the Ohio History Connection*, Wilbur H. Siebert Collection, 25 November 1895.

2. "Death of Eli Rouse." *Bedford Gazette*, 15 April 1892.

3. Henry, Thomas W. Autobiography, p. 19, 42-46.

4. "G. H. Spang's Funeral." *Altoona Tribune,* 21 June 1897, p. 1.

5. Underground Railroad Ride program – Stuckey Farm and Hartley House. *2005 Juneteenth Southcentral PA program.*

6. Records of the County Governments (Microfilm Copies); Series Title: R47-Bedford County Slave Records, *Pennsylvania Historical and Museum Commission;* Harrisburg, PA.

7. *Biographical review: containing life sketches of leading citizens of Bedford and Somerset Counties, Pennsylvania*, Biographical Review Pub. Co., Boston, 1899, P. 252-253

8. Everett Press, *Nancy Watkins Recalls Oppressing Days of Slavery,* 24 January 1936, *p. 2.*

9. Watkins family tree. *Ancestry.com and Findagrave.com.*

10. Love family tree. *Ancestry.com and Findagrave.com.*

11. History of Bedford, Somerset and Fulton Counties, Waterman, 1884, p. 238.

12. Records of the County Governments (Microfilm Copies); Series Title: R47-Bedford County Slave Records, *Pennsylvania Historical and Museum Commission;* Harrisburg, PA.

Anderson family tree. *Ancestry.com.*

13. Hickok. *The Hickok genealogy,* 1938, p.278

14. Siebert. *The Underground Railroad from Slavery to Freedom*, 1898, p.95-96.

15. Sandweiss, Martha A. *Princeton & Slavery Project,* accessed 1 November 2023, https://slavery.princeton.edu/stories/presbyterians-and-slavery%233381.

16. Blockson. *African Amerians in Pennsylvania*, Black Classic Press, 1994.

Switala. *Underground Railroad in Pennsylvania*, 2008. p. 32-33.

17. "U.S., Sons of the American Revolution Membership Application, William F. Barclay 20 March 1914. *Ancestry.com*, https://www.ancestry.com/imageviewer/collections/2204/images/32596_242147-00246?pId=297653.

Barclay family tree. *Ancestry.com.*

18. Hickok. *The Hickok genealogy,* 1938, p.422.

19. Records of the County Governments (Microfilm Copies); Series Title: R47-Bedford County Slave Records, *Pennsylvania Historical and Museum Commission;* Harrisburg, PA.

20. John Watson family tree. *Ancestry.com.*

21. *The Kernel of Greatness*, 1971, p. 74

Bradley, Harriette. *"Black Community Reunion,"* Bedford County Historical Society, 1980.

Switala. *Underground Railroad in Pennsylvania*, 2008. p. 31.

22. "Charles F. Cook letter to Wilbur Siebert." *Courtesy of the Ohio History Connection*, Wilbur H. Siebert Collection, 21 June 1945.

"John E. Cobaugh Civil War Record." *Historical Data Systems.*

23. Gilchrist, Annie. "Down Memory Lane - Our Colored Friends." *Bedford Inquirer*, 21 March 1950, part 1.

24. Mearkle, Kevin. *Civil War Soldiers of Bedford County*, detailed Alphabetical listing.

Family tree information. *Ancestry.com.*

25. *The Kernel of Greatness*, 1971, p. 74-75.

26. "A scene at Bedford Springs." *Civilian and Telegraph*, Cumberland, MD, 11 August 1859, p.3.

27. *The Kernel of Greatness*, 1971, p. 120.

"Death of Rev. John Fidler – A Veteran Gone to Rest." *Everett Press*, 2 October 1891, p.3.

28. Blockson, *The Underground Railroad in Pennsylvania*, 1981, p.141.

The Path to Harpers Ferry went through Bedford – Chapter 14

1. Finkelman, Paul. "A look back on John Brown," *National Archives, Prologue Magazine*, Spring 2011.

Villard. *John Brown, a Biography 1800-1859*, 1910, p.18-25.

2. "John Brown." *Kansas Historical Society*, accessed 20 November 2023, https://www.kshs.org/kansapedia/john-brown/11731.

3. "Kansas-Nebraska Act of 1854." *National Archives,* Milestone Documents, https://www.archives.gov/milestone-documents/kansas-nebraska-act?_ga=2.194834538.659569450.1674675260-1834988356.1674060639.

4. Barry. *Bloody Kansas, 1854-65*, 1972, p.8-12

5. Sanborn, *The life and letters of John Brown,* 1885, p.188-189.

6. Finkelman, Paul. "A look back on John Brown," *National Archives, Prologue Magazine*, Spring 2011.

7. Sanborn. *The life and letters of John Brown*, 1885, p.258-259.

8. Villard. *John Brown, a Biography 1800-1859, 1910*, p.240-249.

9. Finkelman, Paul. "A look back on John Brown," *National Archives, Prologue Magazine*, Spring 2011.

10. Douglass. *Life and times of Frederick Douglass*, 1881, p.278-279.

11. Sanborn, *The life and letters of John Brown*, 1885, p.450.

12. Villard. *John Brown, a Biography 1800-1859, 1910*, p.370-371.

13. "Local and Miscellaneous." *Bedford Gazette,* 04 Nov 1859, p.2.

Villard. *John Brown, a Biography 1800-1859, 1910*, p.401-402.

Sanborn, *The life and letters of John Brown*, 1885, p.258-259.

14. *Bedford Gazette article*, 04 Nov 1859, p.2.

"Old John Brown Plays Billiards." *Bedford Gazette*, 21 September 1906, p.6.

15. "John M. Rouse letter to Wilbur Siebert." *Courtesy of the Ohio History Connection*, Wilbur H. Siebert Collection, 25 November 1895.

16. Klein. *President James Buchanan A Biography,* 1962, p.334.

17. Blackburn, Howard E. *History of Bedford and Somerset Counties*, 1906, p. 376.

"Correspondence." *Bedford County Press*, 27 January 1869, p.2.

18. Douglass, Frederick, *Life and times of Frederick Douglass*, 1881, p.324-325.

19. Sanborn, *The life and letters of John Brown*, 1885, p.521.

20. Villard. *John Brown, a Biography 1800-1859, 1910*, p.426-427.

21. Villard. *John Brown, a Biography 1800-1859, 1910*, p.431.

22. Villard. *John Brown, a Biography 1800-1859, 1910*, p.432-433.

23. Sanborn, *The life and letters of John Brown*, 1885, p.556.

Villard. *John Brown, a Biography 1800-1859, 1910,* p.438.

24. Sanborn. *The life and letters of John Brown*, 1885, p.557-558.

Villard. *John Brown, a Biography 1800-1859, 1910*, p.439-450.

25. Sanborn, *The life and letters of John Brown*, 1885, p.558-559.

Villard. *John Brown, a Biography 1800-1859, 1910*, p.451-452.

26. Villard. *John Brown, a Biography 1800-1859, 1910*, p.453-454.

27. "The Harpers Ferry Invasion as Party Capital." *Richmond Enquirer*, 25 October 1859, p.1.

28. "Jefferson Davis, Remarks to U.S. Senate, 08 December 1859." *Congressional Globe, 36th Congress, Volume 1, p.69.*

29. McPherson, James, *Battle Cry of Freedom*, 1988, p.208-209.

Villard, *John Brown, a Biography 1800-1859,* p.498.

30. Horwitz, Tony, *Midnight Rising,* Henry Holt and Company, 2011, p.254

31. Villard, *John Brown, a Biography 1800-1859*, p.554.

Snake Spring Valley, Woodbury, and Bloomfield Township – Chapter 15

1. *The Kernel of Greatness*, 1971, p. 74.

2. Van Horn. *Bible, Axe and Plow*, 1986, p.126-127.

3. *Biographical Review–Somerset and Bedford Counties*, 1899, p.207

4. Relatives of Kevin Mearkle were previous owners of the Stuckey farm. Family gatherings were

held at the farmhouse in the 1990s and early 2000s. The story of the removable finial and the house being an Underground Railroad station was well known then.

Mearkle, Kevin, *Civil War Soldiers of Bedford County*, 2021

Stuckey family tree. *Ancestry.com*.

5. "Old Keagy Homestead." *Morrisons Cove Herald,* 27 August 1967, p.8.

6. Keagy family tree. *Ancestry.com.*

7. "Church of the Brethren Statements on Slavery." *Church of the Brethren,* July 2008, https://www.brethren.org/peacebuilding/wp-content/uploads/sites/17/2018/09/statements-on-modern-day.pdf.

8. History of Bedford, Somerset, and Fulton Counties, Waterman, 1884, p.350-351.

9. "Colonel James Madara." *Altoona Tribune,* 8 May 1879, p.4.

10. "Emancipation Proclamation Anniversary." *Altoona Tribune*, 2 September 1913, p.1.

11. "William Jackson obituary." *Altoona Tribune*, 26 March 1916, p.3

12. "William Nesbit obituary." *Altoona Tribune*, 28 October 1895, p.5.

13. Gaston, Harriett. "William Nesbit: Blair County's first black civil rights leader 1822 to 1895," 4 February 2022, https://sites.psu.edu/harriettgaston5/2022/02/04/william-nesbit-blair-countys-first-black-civil-rights-leader-1822-to-1895/.

14. Blockson. *African Amerians in Pennsylvania,* 1994, p. 142-143.

Daniel Hale Williams III family tree, *Ancestry.com*.

15. "A Hollidaysburgh Episode of the Days of Slavery (about 1852)," *Courtesy of the Ohio History Connection*, Wilbur H. Siebert Collection, 15 July 2020.

16. Storey. *History of Cambria County, Pennsylvania*, 1907, p.188.

"A Pathway to Freedom." *Altoona Mirror*, 25 June 2011, p.A1.

Blackburn, Howard E. *History of Bedford and Somerset*, 1906, p. 378.

Henry, Thomas W. *Autobiography*, p.19.

Fishertown and Pleasantville – Chapter 16

1. Pinsker. "Vigilance in Pennsylvania: Underground Railroad," *PHMC*, 2000, p. 76-77.

"Anti-Slavery." *Quakers in the World,* https://www.quakersintheworld.org/quakers-in-action/11/-Anti-Slavery.

Janney, *The Doctrines of Elias Hicks volume 4,* 1867, p. 2, https://quaker.org/legacy/pamphlets/hicks.pdf.

2. *History of Bedford and Somerset Counties*, 1906, p. 377.

Map of Bedford County PA. Published by E.L. Walker, 1861.

3. "I.P. Blackburn letter to Wilbur Siebert Jan. 14, 1944." *Courtesy of the Ohio History Connection*, Wilbur H. Siebert Collection.

4. *History of Bedford, Somerset, and Fulton Counties*, Waterman, 1884, p.285.

5. "I.P. Blackburn letter to Wilbur Siebert Jan. 14, 1944." *Courtesy of the Ohio History Connection*, Wil-

bur H. Siebert Collection.

6. *History of Bedford, Somerset, and Fulton Counties*, Waterman, 1884, p.290.

7. "Joseph Penrose letter to I. H. Betz, January 29th, 1904." *Bedford County Historical Society*.

8. McKinney, Justin. "Quakers in the Civil War," *The War Post – Revolutionary and Civil War History*, https://warpost.org/american-civil-war/quakers-in-the-civil-war/.

Penrose family tree. *Ancestry.com*.

9. Mearkle, Kevin. *Civil War Soldiers of Bedford County*, 2021.

Garretson family images and information courtesy of Charles Garretson.

10. Thompson, Robert, "Two Days in April: Breakthrough at Petersburg," *American Battlefield Trust*, https://www.battlefields.org/learn/articles/two-days-april-breakthrough-petersburg.

11. Garretson family information provided by Chuck Garretson.

12. Mearkle, Kevin. *Civil War Soldiers of Bedford County Pennsylvania*, 2021.

13. Blackburn, Howard E. *History of Bedford and Somerset*, 1906, p.377-378.

14. Blackburn, Howard E. *History of Bedford and Somerset*, 1906, p.378.

15. Mearkle, Kevin. *Civil War Soldiers of Bedford County*, 2021.

16. "Benjamin H. Walker Obituary." *Altoona Tribune*, 1896 Mar 28, p.1.

17. *History of Bedford, Somerset, and Fulton Counties*, Waterman, 1884, p.293.

18. "Joseph Penrose letter to I. H. Betz, January 29th, 1904." *Bedford County Historical Society*.

History of Bedford and Somerset Counties, 1906, p. 381-382.

19. Bedford Gazette, Murder in St. Clair, 14 Oct 1864, p.3.

20. "The Commonwealth vs. Trout." *Bedford Inquirer*, 24 Feb 1865, p.2.

21. "I.P. Blackburn letter to Wilbur Siebert Jan. 14, 1944." *Courtesy of the Ohio History Connection*, Wilbur H. Siebert Collection.

22. "Another Locofoco Lie!" *Bedford Inquirer*, 10 Oct 1856, P.2.

23. Storey. *History of Cambria County, Pennsylvania,* 1907, p.188.

History of Bedford and Somerset Counties, 1906, p. 377.

24. "Thomas G. Wright letter by Mary Wright Eaton." Wright Family File, *Bedford County Historical Society.*

The Conclusion – Chapter 17

1. "Recapitulation of the Tables of Population, Nativity, and Occupation." *1860 United States Census Report*, p.598, https://www2.census.gov/library/publications/decennial/1860/population/1860a-46.pdf.

2. Bradley, Harriette. *"Black Community Reunion,"* Bedford County Historical Society, 1980.

Bibliography

Armistead, Wilson. *Life of Anthony Benezet*, Sherman & Company Printers, Philadelphia, 1859.

Barry, James P. *Bloody Kansas, 1854-65; guerrilla warfare delays peaceful American* settlement, Watts Publishing, 1972.

Berlin, Ira. *Generations of captivity: a history of African-American slaves*, The Belknap Press, 2003.

Biographical review: containing life sketches of leading citizens of Bedford and Somerset Counties, Pennsylvania, Biographical Review Pub. Co., Boston, 1899.

Blackburn, Howard E. *History of Bedford and Somerset Counties*, The Lewis Publishing Company, New York & Chicago, 1906.

Blockson, Charles L. *The Underground Railroad in Pennsylvania*, Flame International, Jacksonville, FL, 1981.

Blockson, Charles L. *African Amerians in Pennsylvania,* Black Classic Press, 1994.

Douglass, Frederick, *Life and times of Frederick Douglass*, Park Publishing, Hartford CT, 1881.

Drew, Benjamin. *A North-side View of Slavery*, John P. Jewett and Company, Cleveland, 1856.

Gara, Larry, *The Liberty Line:the Legend of the Underground Railroad,* University of Kentucky Press, 1961.

Greenberg, Ethan, *Dred Scott and the Dangers of a Political Court*, Lexington Books, 2010.

Hall, William M. *Reminiscences and sketches, historical and biographical*, Meyers printing house, Harrisburg, PA, 1890.

Henry, Thomas W. *Autobiography of Rev. Thomas W. Henry of the A.M.E. Church*, Baltimore, 1872, https://docsouth.unc.edu/neh/henry/henry.html.

Hickok, Charles Nelson. *The Hickok genealogy: descendants of William Hickocks of Farmington, Connecticut, with ancestry of Charles Nelson Hickok*, The Tuttle Published Company, 1938, p.278.

History of Bedford, Somerset and Fulton Counties, Pennsylvania, Waterman, Watkins & Co. Chicago, 1884.

Hood J.W. *One hundred years of the African Methodist Episcopal Zion Church*, A.M.E. Zion New York publishing, 1895.

Horwitz, Tony, *Midnight Rising,* Henry Holt and Company, 2011.

Janney, Samuel M. *The Doctrines of Elias Hicks volume 4,* originally published in 1867. https://quaker.org/legacy/pamphlets/hicks.pdf.

Jordan, Philip D. *The National Road*, Boobs-Merrill Company, 1948.

Karns, Charles W. *Historical sketches of Morrisons Cove*, Altoona Mirror Press, 1933.

The Kernel of Greatness: an informal bicentennial history of Bedford County, Bedford County Heritage Commission, Himes Printing Co., 1971.

Klein, Philip Shriver. *President James Buchanan A Biography,* Pennsylvania State University, 1962.

MacCabe, Virginia Parsons. *Parsons' family history and record*, C. W. Nickey Publisher, Decatur IL,

1913.

McPherson, James. *Battle Cry of Freedom,* Oxford University Press, 1988.

Mearkle, Kevin. *Civil War Soldiers of Bedford County Pennsylvania,* IngramSpark, 2021.

Pinsker, Matthew. *Vigilance in Pennsylvania: Underground Railroad Activities in the Keystone State, 1837-1861*, Pennsylvania Historical and Museum Commission, 2000. https://gis.penndot.gov/CRGISAttachments/Survey/2000-H001-042.pdf.

Sanborn, Franklin B. *The life and letters of John Brown, liberator of Kansas, and martyr of Virginia,* Roberts Brothers Publishing, Boston, 1885.

Searight, Thomas B, *The Old Pike, a History of the National Road*, Uniontown - Searight, 1894.

Snowberger, Ella, M. *Recollections of Bygone Days in the Cove*, Morrisons Cove Herald, Volume 7-1939 & volume 8-1940.

Siebert, Wilber H. *The Underground Railroad from Slavery to Freedom,* Macmillan Publishing, New York, 1898.

Storey, Henry Wilson, *History of Cambria County, Pennsylvania*, Lewis Publishing Company, 1907.

Switala, William J. *Underground Railroad in Pennsylvania*, Stackpole Books, 2008.

Van Horn, Ben F. *Bible, Axe and Plow*, Closson Press, 1986.

VanderVelde, Lea, *Mrs. Dred Scott: A Life on Slavery's Frontier,* Oxford Press, 2009.

Villard, Oswald Garrison, *John Brown, 1800-1859; a biography fifty years after*, Houghton Mifflin Company, Boston, 1910.

Wallace, Paul A.W. *Indian Paths of Pennsylvania,* Pennsylvania Historical and Museum Commission, 1965.

Wesley, John. *Thoughts upon Slavery in "A Collection of Religious Tracts,"* Joseph Crukshank publishing, Philadelphia, 1778.

Wilson, Henry. *History of the rise and fall of the slave power in America*, J.R. Osgood and Company, Boston, 1872.

Index

A

abolitionist 12, 19, 29, 33, 57, 61, 62, 73, 76, 78, 81, 82, 89, 96
Adams Sentinel 60, 61, 113
African Episcopal Church of St. Thomas 5
African Methodist Episcopal Church 5, 14, 31, 32, 33, 52, 64, 71, 86, 108, 111, 119
African Methodist Episcopal Zion Church 14, 71, 86, 108, 119
A History of the Negro Troops in the War of the Rebellion 15
Albaugh
  John 89, 90
Alexander
  John 13
Aliquippa 45
Allegheny Mountains 90
Allen
  Avery 89, 100
  Henry T. 16
Allison
  John 94
Altoona 6, 58, 63, 66, 82, 84, 85, 86, 91, 96, 106, 107, 108, 113, 114, 117, 118, 119
Altoona Mirror 82, 108, 117, 119
Altoona Tribune 6, 58, 84, 85, 96, 106, 107, 113, 114, 117, 118
Alum Bank 90, 96, 97, 98
Anderson
  George W. 66, 67, 68, 69
  John 67, 68
  William Watson 14
Andersonville 94
Antietam i, 12, 21
Appalachian Mountains 26
Armstrong
  George 13
Averell
  William 34

B

Bacon
  Dick 100
Bailey 14
Baltimore and Ohio Railroad 23, 25
Barbershops 86
Barclay
  Hugh 10, 68
  Samuel M. 10
Barker
  Abraham Andrews 86, 87, 100
Barks
  Alfred 16
  Carrie and Susan 15, 59
  Henry 15, 56, 58, 59, 108, 113
  John R. 16
  Moore 16
  William Tecumseh 15, 16, 59

Barndollar
  Catherine 48, 49, 50
  Eliza Ellis 48
  Jacob T. 48, 49, 50, 52, 53
  Jacob W. 50, 51
  James E. 50
  James J. 50
  James M. 48, 49
  John 51
  John W. 50
  Martin D. 50, 52
  Mary 51
  Michael 45, 47, 48, 52
  Peter 47, 48
  William 48, 112
  William G. 50
  William P. 50
Barndollar tannery weigh station 49, 53
Barnett
  William 100
Barnhart
  Abraham 63
  Adam 100
  Samuel 100
Barns
  Robert 16
Bates
  Thomas 16
Battle of the Crater 62
Baughman
  Jon 38, 41
Beans Cove 37
Bedford County Area Map 35
Bedford County Historical Society ii, 11, 14, 15, 57, 69, 82, 88, 95, 100, 103, 107, 108, 112, 113, 115, 118, 121
Bedford Gazette ii, 6, 13, 14, 15, 17, 19, 20, 21, 34, 38, 53, 64, 75, 99, 106, 107, 108, 109, 111, 113, 114, 116, 118
Bedford House 57
Bedford Inquirer 19, 20, 59, 60, 63, 64, 70, 99, 109, 111, 113, 115, 118
Bedford Springs Hotel 15, 26, 67, 70, 75, 94, 115
Benezet
  Anthony 5, 106, 119
Berry
  John W. 16
Betz
  I. H. 91, 97, 118
Bible, Axe and Plow 81, 106, 116, 120
Big Dipper 29
Blackburn
  Hiram 91
  Isaiah P. 89, 90, 99
  James 45, 46, 90, 91, 99
  Joseph 94
  Levi 94
  Martin 94
Black Log Valley 27
Black Valley 26, 27, 37, 45, 47, 81

Black Valley Road 37, 45, 47
Blair
  S.S. 84
Blair County 56, 63, 64, 85, 86, 103, 117
Blairsville 59, 113
Bleeding Kansas 73
Bloomfield Furnace 81, 84
Bloomfield Nursery 83
Boaston family 51
Bolden
  Elijah 16
Border Ruffians 73, 74
Boston
  James 16
  John 16
Bowen
  Benjamin 91
Bradley
  David ii, 38
  David H. ii
  Harriette ii, 38, 47, 55, 101
Brady
  Sam 66
Brady Plantation 66
Breckinridge
  John 21
Brethren Church 76, 82, 117
Brice
  John 16
Broad Top Bulletin 38, 111
Brown
  David 84, 85
  George 60, 61
  Henry 16
  James 60
  John 2, 15, 16, 31, 33, 63, 64, 71, 72, 73, 74, 75, 76, 77, 78, 79, 90, 115, 116, 120
  Moses 15
  Perry 15
  Robert 15
  Todd 16
Bruce
  Thomas 13
Bruce Fisher 17
Buchanan
  James 70, 74, 75, 77, 116, 119
Buel
  Hillhouse 26, 31, 110
Burgess 14, 15
Burk
  Cory S. 16
  Thomas 16
Byers
  Peter 16

C

Callahan
  James 16
Cambria County 47, 64, 100, 103, 114, 117, 118, 120
Canada 5, 6, 30, 38, 43, 46, 56, 57, 58, 59, 63, 64, 70, 71, 74, 75, 81, 84, 85, 86, 94
Carns
  Pade 100
Carr
  Sidney 86
  Snyder 59, 86
Carson
  John 16
Carter
  Thomas O.B. 13, 56, 62
Carter Plantation 13, 56, 60, 61, 62, 66
Catfish Ridge 81, 82, 85
Center County 46, 91, 92, 95
Cessna
  Howard 61
Chambersburg 4, 15, 33, 34, 74, 76, 81
Chaneysville Incident 38
Chesapeake & Ohio Canal 23, 25, 26, 32, 105, 109, 110
Chimney Rocks 84, 85, 86
Church Revival 13
Civilian and Telegraph newspaper 70
Claysburg 90
Clearfield County 90
Cobaugh
  George 69, 70
  John 69
Coffin
  Levi vi
Coleman
  George 16
College of Charleston Libraries 4
Compston
  John 45
Conestoga Wagon 23, 24
Copperheads 18, 21, 99
Cosler
  William 15
Costler
  John 16
  Joseph 16
Coulter
  Thomas 13
Cover i, 89, 100
Craft
  Ellen 25
  William 25
Craig
  Mehalla 66
Crawford
  Henry 15
  Jesse R. 58
Crawley
  John 15
  Joseph 15, 63, 64, 65, 75, 86, 96
Crissman 97, 98
Cumberland, Maryland Area Map 28
Cushon
  John 100
Cypher 86, 95

D

Davids
  Tice 5
Davis
  DeCharmes 14, 16, 57
  James 16
  Jefferson 78, 116
  John 16
  Mariah Cooper 14, 57
  Nelson 14, 56, 57
  Richard 15
Davison
  Lewis 13
Dean
  Andrew 13, 16
  Jacob 16
  John 13
Democratic Enquirer 6, 7
Deuteronomy 23:15-16 36
Dicken
  Jacob 56, 57
Dickinson College 11, 107
Dom
  Harriet Griffin 38
Doogen
  Henry 16
Doran
  Thomas 68, 69
Dougherty
  Bernard 13
Douglas
  Stephen 20, 73
Douglass
  Frederick 12, 29, 73, 74, 76, 110, 115, 116, 119
Dred Scott Decision 2, 10
Drinking Gourd 29, 110
Dunkle's Barber Shop 47
Dunning's Creek 89
Dunnings Creek Friends Museum 97, 100
Duvall
  Jeremiah 13

E

Eastern Lights Cemetery 66
East Freedom 90
Eaton
  Mary Wright 100, 118
Ebensburg 86, 87, 100
Edwards
  Amos 100
  Josiah 95
Election of 1860 20
Election of 1864 22
Ely
  Constable 8
Emancipation Proclamation 12, 21, 117
Emmanuel Parish of the Episcopal 31, 32, 105, 110
Eshleman
  David D. 76
Esrey
  Moses 70

Everett Press 57, 105, 112, 113, 114, 115
Evitts Mountain 14, 26, 37, 47, 55
Exchange Hotel 86

F

Ferguson
  John 13
Fidler
  John 2, 15, 56, 57, 58, 63, 64, 65, 75, 76, 86, 91, 96, 105, 113, 115
Fisher
  Jacob 90
Fishertown Brethren Cemetery 76
Flintstone 5, 24, 26, 27, 37
Flintstone Hotel 24, 37
Fockler
  Sally Barndollar 50, 51
Folck's Mill 34
Forbes Road 45
Fortune
  Wallace 100
Fourney's Press 70
Frank Leslie's Illustrated Newspaper 11, 78
Franklin
  Benjamin 22
Fredericksburg 50, 51
Frederick Town Herald 5, 6, 106
Friends 70, 91, 93, 94, 97, 100, 115
Friends Cemetery 91, 93, 94
Fruit Hill farm 45
Fry
  Henry 16
  John 16
  Nelle 47, 48, 50, 52
Fryle 14
Fugitive Slave Act of 1793 9
Fugitive Slave Act of 1850 1, 6, 10
Fugitive Slave Law 56, 59, 63, 70
Fulton County 61, 90, 91, 96

G

Galbraith
  Ellen 60, 61
Gallitzin 86, 87
Gant
  Richard 6, 7
Ganz
  Thomas 16
Garretson
  Benjamin H. 93, 94
  Josiah P. 93
  Thomas 95
Garrison
  William Lloyd 61, 78
Gates
  Benjamin 15
  George 15
  Reuben 15, 16
Geistown 47, 86, 90, 91, 100
Germany Valley Cemetery 76

Gettys
  Thomas R. 60, 61, 113
Gibson
  John 16
God 6, 10, 19, 52, 67, 74
Good
  William 15
Gordon
  Catherine 16
  Daniel 16
  Orange 66
  William 15
Gradual Abolition Act of 1780 9, 14, 50, 65, 106, 112
Graham
  James 69, 70, 86
  Mary Cosler 69, 70
Granger
  Gordon 12
Grant
  Ulysses S. 12
Gravel Hill 64, 71
Great Compromise 10
Green
  Jackson 15, 66, 67
  Jacob 58, 59, 86
Greystone Hotel 17
Griffin
  Nora Imes 38
Grove house 68, 69, 88
Gump
  George W. 21
  John A. 21
  Sophia Stuckey 21

H

Habeas corpus 8, 56, 63
Hafer
  Colonel 75
Hall
  William Maclay 3, 19, 47, 55
Hamilton
  Richard 15
Hammond
  E. 8
  Essington 84
  Nathan 90
Hammond Hill 90
Harbaugh
  Eli 94, 96
  Emanuel 94
  George 90, 95, 96
  George W. 94, 96
  Jason 95
  John 94, 96
  Joseph 95
  Nancy (Minnie) Edwards 96
  Robert 94, 96
  William H. 95
  Wilson 94, 95
Harpers Ferry v, 2, 14, 31, 33, 64, 73, 75, 76, 77, 78, 79, 90, 115, 116
Harper's Weekly 18
Harris
  Amos 15, 41
  Charles 15
  James 24, 110
  John T. 16
  Joshua 16
Harris Hotel 17, 71
Hartley
  Eliza 68
  John 63
  John G. 64, 65
  William 16, 65
Hedges
  Martha 48
Helsop 89, 100
Hemming
  William 60
Henry
  Henry 100
  James 33
  Thomas W. 32, 33, 64, 86, 111, 119
Herald of Freedom & Torch Light 4, 60, 113
Heslop
  Mr. and Mrs. James 100
Hess
  George 100
  Samuel 100
  Samuel, George, and John 90
Hewit
  Major 84
Hickhok Genealogy Book 67, 68, 69
Hicks
  Elias 89, 117, 119
Hicksite Quakers 89
History of Bedford, Somerset, and Fulton Counties 67, 90, 97, 98, 112, 116, 117, 118, 119
History of the Negro Race in America from 1619 to 1880 15
Hollidaysburg 6, 8, 10, 33, 58, 59, 64, 81, 82, 84, 85, 86, 90, 95
Hollidaysburg Union Cemetery 86
Hollinger
  James 13
  Stephen 16
Holmes
  Philip 16
Holsinger
  Frank 16
Huddleson
  Jonathan 37
Huntingdon County 27

I

Iames 38, 41, 42
  Alton 38
  William 41, 42
Iams
  William 42
Imboden

John D. 59
Imes
  Aaron 42
  Lester 38, 43
  Upton 41
Imes Cemetery i, 39, 40
Imler
  Thomas C. 38
Indentured servitude 9

J

Jackson
  Stonewall 79
  William 85, 117
Jameson
  Rachel 68
Jansens Farm supply 47
Jayhawkers 73
Jeffries
  Howard B. 16
Johnson
  David 16
  Moses 16
  William 15, 16
Johnstown 45, 46, 47, 65, 69, 89, 96, 97, 100, 112, 113
Johnstown Road 45, 97
Jordan
  Bill 38
Jordon
  Henry 16
Juneteenth 12, 47, 48, 112, 114

K

Kagi
  John Henrie 75
Kansas-Nebraska Act of 1854 73, 115
Kaylor
  Frederick 100
Keagy
  Jacob H. 82, 83
Keagy homestead 81, 82
Kennedy
  James H. 9
Kernel of Greatness 6, 115, 116, 119
Key
  James 16
  Philip 16
Kirk
  William 76, 90
Knaugel House 71
Knisley
  Wilda Iames 41
Krausen
  E.W. 16

L

Lafayette 76
Lee
  Robert E. 12, 77, 93
Lemon
  Samuel and Jean 86
Lemon House Tavern 86, 87
Lewis
  Bert 16
  George 14
  George T. 16
  Lindsay 61
  Robert 16
  Robert M. 16
Liberator
  abolitionist newspaper 61, 62, 114
Library of Congress 12, 14, 17, 18, 24, 72, 74, 77, 79, 109, 110
Licking Creek 61
Lincoln
  Abraham 10, 12, 19, 20, 79, 92
Lisles
  George 16
Lloyd
  Sarah Barndollar 48
Lost Run 37
Love
  Chauncey 13
  Delilah 60
  George 16, 59, 60
  John 13, 60, 65, 66, 71
  John R. 16
  Mary 6
Low 86, 95
Lucas
  Peyton 29, 30
Luckett
  Alexander 16
Lumac
  William 16
Luskey
  Samuel 46
Lutheran Church 82
Lyles
  David 16
  George 16
  James 16
Lyons
  Benjamin 14
  George W. 14, 16
  James H. 14

M

Madera
  James 81, 83
Magraw
  P. M. 71
Marshall
  Ann Elizabeth 16
  Harry 56, 57
  Martin 16
Martin 13, 15, 16, 50, 52, 94
  Charles 13
Martin Barndollar family photograph 52

Maryland Advocate 6, 7, 106
Maryland Center for History and Culture 25
Mason-Dixon line 6, 30, 32, 37, 41, 55, 56
Maxwell
  Edward 45
McCausland
  John 34
McClellan
  George 12, 22
McConnellsburg 34
McLain
  William "Mose" 100
McPherson
  Cyrus 16
  John 16
Meadowbrook Terrace 57
Methodist Church 5, 14, 31, 32, 52, 65, 112, 119
Mexican War 15
Meyers
  Benjamin F. 75
Miller
  Barbara Sponsler 49, 52, 53, 103, 112
  Charles W. 16
  David 16
  Eli 89, 90, 95, 100
  Mark 88, 89, 100
  Mary Calhoun 88
  Thomas 89
  William H. 94, 95
Mingo 13
Missouri Compromise of 1820 73
Mitchel family 56, 59
Mock
  Frederick 99
  William Roy 94, 96, 97, 100, 103
Monroe
  James 10
  S. 75
Moor
  Robert 13
Moore
  John Jamison 14
Moorefield 34
Morgan
  Margaret 9
Morgart
  Elizabeth Beegle 54
  John Cessna 54, 55, 113
  Patricia 49, 103
  William 55
Morgart Tavern 54
Morrisons Cove Herald 50, 82, 112, 117, 120
Mother Bethel African Methodist Episcopal 5
Mount Miserable Hill 88, 89
Mount Olivet Cemetery 82
Mount Union Cemetery 94
Mt. Pisgah A.M.E. church 52
Mt. Ross Cemetery 56, 70, 126
Murdoch
  Francis B. 10, 11
Myers
  John 100

N

National Road 23, 24, 25, 34, 37, 105, 109, 111, 119, 120
Nawgle
  Frederick and Eve 71
Negro Knob 14
Negro Road 27
Nesbit
  William W. 63, 64, 85, 86, 96, 117
New Buena Vista 14
Norris
  Edward 15
  Martha 56
North Star v, 29, 94, 110

O

Old Bedford Pike 97
Old Conemaugh Path 97
Old Johnstown Road 97
Old Presbyterian Cemetery 64, 68
Osawatomie 73, 74, 77
Ott
  Mike 51
Over
  David 19

P

Parker
  James 16
Parson
  James 58
Patrick and Abraham 44, 45, 46, 47, 90
Paynes
  George 13
Peace Democrats 12, 21
Pendergrass
  Garrett 13
Pennsylvania Historical and Museum Commission 26, 48, 65, 95, 112, 114, 115, 120
Pennsylvania Personal Liberty Law of 1826 9, 60, 107
Penn West Hotel 71
Penrose
  Amos 91, 92
  Amos and Sophia 91
  Hester Lucretia Mock 92
  James married Anne 91
  Joseph 91, 92, 93, 94, 97, 118
  Josiah and Samuel 91
  Samuel and Josiah 90
  William and Thomas 91
Perry
  Wyatt 16, 56, 57, 59, 62, 69, 113
Pioneer Historical Society 38, 111
Piper
  John 37
  Watson J. 37
Piper hotel 37
Pittsburgh Gazette 70

Plowden
  Jacob 16
  John C. 16
Poplar Grove house 68
Popular sovereignty 73
Potomac River 23, 25, 26, 29, 31, 33, 34, 76
Pottawatomie Massacre 73
Presbyterian Church 67
Prigg
  Edward 9
Prigg v. Pennsylvania 9, 107

Q

Quaker 2, 5, 14, 46, 47, 63, 89, 90, 91, 93, 94, 95, 96, 97, 100, 117, 118
Quaker Valley 90

R

Rainsburg Seminary 48
Rays Hill 27
Reed
  Louis 16
Revolutionary War 9, 10, 13, 22, 45, 68
Richmond Inquirer 78
Robinson
  Mary 13
  Thomas 37
Rocky Gap 37
Rohm
  Conrad 60, 61, 113
Romney, West Virginia 13, 14, 58, 59
Rose
  William 13
Rouse
  Elias 63, 64, 65, 75, 76, 86, 96
  John W. vi, 56, 63, 75, 76
Route 40 23, 24
Rush
  Benjamin 5, 106

S

Saltpetre Cave 37
Schell
  William P. 17
Schoenberger
  Peter 82
Scott
  Dred 2, 10, 11, 107, 119, 120
  Harriet Robinson 10
Second Great Awakening 13
Semmes
  Samuel 31
Shell
  William P. 6
Shenandoah Valley 12, 34
Sheridan
  Philip 12
Sherman
  William Tecumseh 12
Sherrard
  John 45
Shobers Run 69
Showmo 86, 95
Shriver Ridge gap 26
Siebert
  Wilbur H. vi, 1, 56, 63, 89, 99, 113, 114, 115, 116, 117, 118
Slaughter
  Jesse 13
Slave pass 4, 57
Sleek (also spelled Slick) 91
  Samuel A. 100
  William 46, 47, 89, 90, 94
Slick
  Josiah 16
  William 86, 100
Smith
  Isaac 75
  John 75
  Nancy 65
  Patrick 6
  Samuel 16
Snowberger
  Ella M. 50
  Jacob 14
Somerset 34, 49, 65, 67, 69, 70, 84, 90, 91, 96, 97, 98, 105, 107, 108, 112, 113, 114, 116, 117, 118, 119
Spang
  George H. 60, 63
Sparks
  Ronnie 41
Speer 61
Spriggs 6, 8
Spring Meadow 91, 93, 94
Spurgeon
  James 41
St. Clairsville 45, 46, 47
St. Clair Township 20, 35, 46, 47, 76, 89, 90, 96, 97, 99, 100, 112
Stewart
  Jeb 77
  Preston 13, 16, 108
Strathers
  James 16
  Willis 16
Streets
  James 16
  Nancy 66
  Rankin 16
Stuckey
  Asa Silver 80, 81
  John S. 82
Stuckey farm 81, 82, 116
Stump
  George W. 59
Swartz
  John 16

T

Taliaferro
  Eliza Dillon 10, 107
  Lawrence 10, 11, 107
Tannery Weigh Station 47
Tate
  Joseph 63, 64
The Last Station: Underground Railroad of Quaker Corner 100
Thirteenth Amendment 12
Thoreau
  Henry David 79
Tillman 13, 16
  George 16
  Isaac 16
  Jackson 16
Tobias
  John B. 16
Tolar
  Daniel 13
Town Creek 37, 38, 39, 40, 41, 43
Trout
  Gideon D. 99
  James 99
Tucker
  J. Randolph 59
Tussey
  Betsy 45

U

Union Hotel 47
U.S.C.T. 14, 15, 16, 56, 57, 60, 62, 66, 70

V

Van Horn
  Ben F. 81
Vigilance Committee of Philadelphia 4

W

Walker
  Abner 96
  Asahel, Benjamin and Morris 95
  Benjamin H. 2, 63, 64, 89, 90, 92, 94, 95, 96, 97, 100, 118
  Isaac, Mary Minerva, and Midge 94
  Morris 86, 95
  Rebecca 100
  Thomas G. 94
  William A. 94
Wallace 15, 100, 110, 120
Warren
  Nathan 13
  Nimrod 16, 61
Warriors Paths 26, 27
Washington
  George 5, 15, 17, 76, 106, 108
  Lewis 76, 78
Watkins
  Hiram 16
  Nancy 16, 65, 114
Watson
  John 68, 69, 115
  William H. 55
  William, I. 14, 68
Way
  Cyrus 91
  David 91
  Hiram 88, 89
  Samuel 88, 89, 90, 91
Waynesburg 45
Weatherington
  Isaac 100
Webber
  Charles vi
Wedley
  Charles 61
Wesley
  John 52
Western Maryland Historical Library 4, 7, 23, 24, 26, 110
Whitman
  Walt 79
Whitney
  Eli 43
Willard
  Lewis 16
Williams
  Catherine Barndollar 49
  Daniel Hale 86, 87, 117
  George Washington 15, 16, 17, 64, 108
  Henry 55
  Henry S. 16
  Jacob Barndollar 50
  John H. 50
  Samuel 48, 49, 50
  Samuel D. 50
Wills Creek 26, 31
Wilson
  Henry W. 16
  John 15
Wise
  Eric 43
Wright
  Thomas G. 100, 118
  William 100

Y

Yingling
  Laurie Ann 48
Young
  Aaron 16, 70
  Daniel D. 16
  Jacob 16, 70
  Jacob P. 16
  Lydia 16
  Peter 16
Young butcher shop 71

Z

Zimmerman Hardware building 47, 50

www.ingramcontent.com/pod-product-compliance
Lightning Source LLC
Chambersburg PA
CBHW061129170426
43209CB00014B/1713